OPENING THE BOX
The Popular Experience of Television

Edited by
Ian Clayton,
Colin Harding
&
Brian Lewis

YORKSHIRE ART CIRCUS

NATIONAL MUSEUM
PHOTOGRAPHY · FILM · TELEVISION
PICTUREVILLE · BRADFORD

1995

Published jointly by Yorkshire Art Circus, School Lane Castleford WF10 4QH, and the National Museum of Photography, Film & Television, Pictureville, Bradford BD1 1NQ

Distributed by Yorkshire Art Circus, Glasshoughton Cultural Industries School Lane, Castleford WF10 4QH
© Text - Yorkshire Art Circus and the National Museum of Photography, Film & Television
© Photographs - National Museum of Photography, Film & Television and contributors

Technical Co-ordinator:
Reini Schühle

Editorial and Research Team:
Phil Paver, Rebecca Roe.

Design and Technical Team:
Bob Cox, Jane Crumack, Pam Oxley,
Paul Thompson

Printed by:
Thornton and Pearson Ltd., Rosse Street, Thornton Road Bradford BD8 9AS

ISBN 1 898311 15 3

Classification: Television/General Interest

Yorkshire Art Circus is a registered charity No 1007443 supported by:
Yorkshire and Humberside Arts
West Yorkshire Grants
Wakefield MDC

The NMPFT is part of the National Museum of Science & Industry

Cover illustration:
Postcard c.1955, Artist Bob Wilkin, Publisher unknown.
There's nothing like a nice holiday for a complete change.

FOREWORD

Yorkshire Art Circus is a unique book publisher,
bringing to all members of its community the opportunity
to write about their lives and experiences, and to put them in print.
The National Museum of Photography, Film and Television is a unique museum,
interpreting for everyone the media which form part of all our lives.
With such complementary aims, it is almost inevitable -
and entirely logical - that these two Yorkshire institutions
should become partners.

In 1992 we looked at the popular
experience of photography and, by getting people to write and talk
about their family photographs, produced *Kept In A Shoebox*,
a prize-winner in the prestigious Raymond Williams community
publishing competition organised by the Arts Council.

The following year we turned our attention to cinema-going.
The resulting book, *Talking Pictures*, explored the popular experience
of the cinema.

With this look at television, we complete our trilogy of books on the
popular experience of the media. Television-watching is often criticised
as being a totally passive experience.
This varied collection of memories, anecdotes and opinions shows, however,
that this is by no means the case.

Amanda Nevill, National Museum of Photograhy, Film & Television
Brian Lewis, Yorkshire Art Circus

INTRODUCTION

I was born in 1936 the very year when Baird was experimenting with the earliest broadcasts, and possibly conceived on the very day he was sending the first signals from London to a friend's house in Leeds. As I grew up, I became a wireless and News Theatre fan, but as time passed I became more and more aware that Londoners were watching television but we in the Midlands were not. Then the communications and entertainments revolution reached Birmingham.

I can remember the mast going up at Sutton Coldfield and then the cultural explosion as new programmes became the talking point of every factory canteen and bus stop. In those early days as mast after mast began transmitting and yet there was only one programme, the nation was culturally united as it has rarely been since. Naturally there was opposition.

Quickly television became the goggle box, or as one school teacher always called it- the idiots lantern, before settling down and becoming simply the box.

The Suez crisis was the first war I watched on the box, in this case a large television set standing in the centre of the NAAFI at RAF Topcliffe. I watched "Coronation Street" when Ena Sharples was the star and admired Honor Blackman, Joanna Lumley and Diana Rigg in "The Avengers". In 1971 I got my BA by scheduling my life around a number of intellectual programmes transmitted by the Open University and once met a man who was being paid to set up a new programme called "Channel Four". I have wept over the Biafra and Ethiopian famines, laughed with Harry Worth and Lenny Henry, been appalled by the mediocrity of Larry Grayson and experimented by watching World Championship Snooker in black and white; by far the most interesting way of watching the sport, closed meetings early so that the committee could get home to watch "Cracker".

Some things I have not done. I have not bought Sky so that I could watch Italian housewives take their clothes off in television game shows, telephoned in to vote on a current affairs programme, seen Princess Di weep to camera, kept the television on when visitors called, thought that Oprah Winfrey was especially relevant, or decided to put one in the kitchen so that I could view as I cooked.

Everybody has a life story in television which runs parallel to their biological one and people who were born after 1960 have probably spent more time watching than they have bathing, eating and making love, and it is getting worse. I'm old enough to remember when there wasn't a television set in our house, though not old enough to remember when there wasn't a radio, so I have a start. It is sobering to think that by the time today's teenagers reach maturity, many will have watched more television than they have had hours of sleep.

Television shapes people every bit as much as diet or muscle toning does, yet despite this there have been few books which consider this massive cultural revolution from the consumers point of view and hardly any which are based on people's views and experiences of television.

Brian Lewis

We should like to thank the following people for sharing their stories and photographs:

Pat Ackroyd, Ray Ackroyd, Jean Aldersea, J Alderson, Lena Allen, Gina Alliston, Jan Astin, Mary Astin, Elsie Baker, Alex Banwell, Laura Banwell, Jennifer Barraclough, Joyce Baulch, Mrs S R Beckwith, Hafsa Begum, M Bennett, Nora Bennett, Joan Berriman, Jason Bentley, Kev Beverage, Mrs I Bostock, Peter Boswell, Diane Bower, Constance Boyle, Ruth Boyle, Diane Brewster, G Briant, Doreen Brookfield, Sidney Brown, Joan Bruce, Carol Bullock, Maureen Burland, Joan Burley, B M Burrows, C J Burrows, Stephen P Bush, Maureen Butterworth, Ronnie Calleja, Jerry Caplan, J H Carroll, R Caunt, Tony Champion, Stanley Claughton, Ian Clayton, Mrs G Cooper, Mrs K Cooper, Sylvian Coulson, Mrs P Cowling, Wendu Clegg, Bob Cox, Frances Cox, G J Cuckson, Sylvia Curley, Nigel Davies, Roy Dennison, A Dobson, Vikki Douthwaite, Florence Dunn, J Edmonds, Wilfred Ellis, Andrew Emmerson, Elizabeth Emmott, Nicola Evans, W G Evans, John Evison, Lynn Firth, Sylvia Ford, Olive Fowler, J R Fox, B Gantan, Jo Gilbert, Roy Gilbert, Gwen Gragg, Howard Greenfield, Kathleen Gresswell, A J Griffin, Joyce Haigh, Harry Haley, Doris Halliwell, Mrs J Hart, Dorothy Hempel, Carol Hersee, Evelyn Hodson, T E Hodson, W Holden, P J Hood, Mildred Horsley, Eva Howard, Dicky Howett, P C Hoyes, Andrea Hoyland, Reginald Hughes, Ian Hutcheon, Neil Johnson, Chris Jones, M Jones, Poppy Jones, Sarandeep Kaila, Kaktus, Mary Kelsey, Adinder Khan, Ian Kilburn, Geoff King, Dave Lawton, Bill Leach, Alan Lester, Jacob Lewis, Malcolm Lewis, J Machen, Mrs A M Mallinson, Ruth Maltby, Miss B Marshall, Mary Mason, Alison Maud, A M Mauwson, Eric Midgeley, Mavis Midgeley, Zoe Mockford, Joy Moses, George Munson,

James Marcus, Paul Murphy, Peter and Yvonne Murphy, Mrs G M Norris, Audrey Ogg, Bernard Owen, Rachel Oxtoby, C A Painter, Vera Palmer, Heather Parkinson, Phil Paver, T Perry, Dr W Pickin, May Pickles, Margaret Pilkington, Rachel Pocock, Mrs J K Potts, David Pratt, Stephen C Pratt, Ron Priestley, Janet Pringle, Mrs J Pullan, Mr & Mrs K E Pryke, Muriel Ragis, Dennis Ramm, Rebecca Ramm, Kathleen Ramsey, Joan Reeves, E Rhodes, Laurence Richardson, P Robertson, John Robinson, Rebecca Roe, Gladys Rooker, Paul Rowe, Rebecca Rowe, Sylvia Roye, Peter A Rushforth, P W Sanderson, Paul Sawtell, Elisabeth Schühle, Helmut Schühle, Kristina Schühle, Neils Schühle, Uli Schühle, Louisa Shaw, Sheila Skelding, Wilton C Smith, Rod Souler, Judy Spencer, A F Sumner, M Sutherland, Joan Sykes, Daisy Tempest, Peter Thody, J Thomas, A Thompson, Rhona Tiernan, Margaret Tomlinson, Jack Townend, Matthew Troth, Janet P Turner, Kathleen Turner, Jean Tyler, L Tyler, Kathryn Vale, Sheena Vigors, Carl Waite, Kim Ward, Kenneth Watkins, Linda Watkins, M Weeks, Gerald Wells, Peter West, Mrs H White, Chris Whitefield, Tracey Whitton, Joanne Widdop, F C Willis, S Willis, Don Wilson, Graham Wood, Mike Woods, Gerry Woodgate, Christine Wraith, Mrs Wriglesworth, Ian Potter, Virginia Ironside, Keith Hamer.

We should also like to thank:
405 Alive
Test Card Circle
Vintage Wireless Museum
Christopher Pratt's
TV Licensing

CHAPTER ONE

JUST LIKE ONE OF THE FAMILY

BAIRD TELEVISOR, 1930.
The Baird Televisor was the first television set anywhere in the world to be offered for sale to the public. Manufactured by Plessey, they went on sale in February, 1930, costing 25 guineas. Even with a magnifying lens, the picture was only about the size of a large postage stamp. Since the image was composed only of thirty lines picture definition was very poor. A second wireless set was needed in order to receive the accompanying sound broadcast.

PHILIP'S PROJECTION TELEVISION, 1938.
Projection televisions were at the top of the range of pre-war models. A variant of standard sets, these projected a picture on to a translucent screen. By this means, a much bigger picture could be produced - this model gave a picture 18" by 14 1/2". Because of their very high prices (this model cost 120 guineas) very few projection sets were sold.

MARCONIPHONE 702 MIRROR-LID TELEVISION, 1937.
In their quest for larger picture sizes, manufacturers used larger cathode ray tubes. These had the drawback, however, of being very long. A twelve-inch tube was about three feet long. In order to fit this into a cabinet without making it too big for the average room, it was mounted vertically. The screen was then viewed via a mirror on the under-side of a lid which opened at a 45% angle. With the lid closed, the set looked just like an ordinary radiogram.

BUSH TV22, 1950.
With its characteristic styling and bakelite cabinet, the TV22 has become an icon of the 1950s. With the opening of the BBC's regional transmitters after 1949, televisions were sold that were permanently tuned into the local wavelength. Manufacturers produced distinct 'London' and 'Birmingham' versions of each of their models. The TV22 was the first receiver that the user could themselves tune to any of the five 'Band 1' channels on which the BBC was to build up its national network.

EKCO PORTABLE TELEVISION, MODEL TMB272, 1955.
One of the first portable sets, the TMB272 had a 9" screen. As well as a television it was also a VHF radio. For mobility it coud be run off a 12-volt battery. Its power consumption, however, was very heavy. After a pleasant evening's viewing, one group of people on a motor yacht found themselves drifting at sea because they were unable to start the engine.

HOME-MADE TELEVISION SET, 1955.
After the Second World War, although prices were gradually falling, the cost of a new television set was still too much for many people. Knowledgable enthusiasts often built their own televisions using cheap surplus radio and radar equipment. To make the job easier, televisions were also sold in kit-form, using a combination of commercial and ex-government components. The quality of picture obtained with these sets was often comparable to shop-bought models. In 1948 it was estimated that 3% of all televisions in use in Britain were home-made.

SINCLAIR MICROVISION, 1966.
First shown at the 1966 Television and Radio Show, held at Earls Court, the Sinclair Microvision used a specially developed 2" cathode ray tube. In 1982, Sinclair went on to develop his flat-screen TV, the world's first truly miniature pocket television.

PERDIO 'PORTARAMA', 1961.
At first, television sets used valves. From the mid-1950s, however, transistors began to replace valves in radios. Perdio (from 'personal radio') was formed in 1955 and specialised in the manufacture of portable transistor radios. In 1961, after much development work, they introduced the 'Portarama'. Advertised as 'a real go-anywhere TV', this was the world's first all-transistor television set.

SONY KV 1320 TRINITRON COLOUR TELEVISION, 1971.
In the 1960s and 1970s British television manufacturers faced growing competition from the Far East. The KV 1320 was the first Japanese set to be sold in large quantities in Britain. Although colour sets were initially much more expensive than monochrome ones, the public's appetite for colour pictures was not to be denied. In 1968 there were just 20,000 colour sets in use. By 1978 the number had risen to eleven million.

The National Radio Exhibition, Olympia 1936.
A Radiolympia Girl holding a cathode ray tube.

CHAPTER TWO
CORONATION STREET

․ Everybody tells you that their family first got a television to watch the Coronation. Ours didn't. Not a chance - we hadn't enough money. Dad was a royalist, so the only place to be on Coronation Day was London. He decided to make it a bit of a holiday. Mom had met a Cockney couple on a holiday somewhere or other and they had got on well, so we went down to London - to the centre of things. I'd be eight. It seemed that everyone was intent on going to the capital. The trains were full and there were Union Jacks everywhere. This was the new Elizabethan Age. Everest had been climbed two days earlier. We were passing from one historic period to another. Dad, however, was a bit timid. Mom didn't fancy all the crowds and, in any case, the weather was cold and damp. In the end we settled for home comforts and, in a room filled with Woodbine smoke, watched the crowning of the monarch on Alf and Lil's television in an upstairs flat somewhere at the back of Walworth Road, Elephant and Castle. A mile across the river, outside Westminster Abbey, city gents threw damp bowler hats into the air in celebration.

․ The back-to-back terrace houses of Carlisle Street, Hunslet, were one up and one down; living room on the ground floor and bedroom above - both rooms only four yards by three yards. The weather was atrocious and everyone who lived in the street was crowded into the small room to see the Queen crowned. Children sat on the floor, almost up to the screen. Grown-ups stood around the walls. Some even sat on the door step. The coach approached Westminster Abbey. We were all spellbound. A mounted cavalry man on his horse blocked the screen. All we could see was the rear end of the horse. My sister, who was Downs Syndrome, said "Shift" and rubbed the screen with the hem of her dress. Miraculously, when her dress went down, we were just in time to see the Queen step out of the coach. "That's better", she said. Even today, when we watch something we say, "Wipe it off", as she believed all her life that this was all she had to do if she didn't like the programme. Wouldn't it be lovely if we could do that now?

․ We had our first set, a Murphy 12" rented at 8/11d per week, in 1953, but not until the Autumn of that year. I was fourteen and desperate to 'view' the Coronation in the June. The "Birmingham Mail" was offering seats in the Town Hall to view the television pageant, a whole day's viewing on eight huge projectors. Being enterprising, I managed to secure two tickets for myself and a pal. It was an exciting affair, the hall was packed and much excitement was generated. Viewers were quiet in those days, being practised in cinema "hush"! There was much awe and respect - all very memorable. Later, we had a street party and a knees-up!

․ There were surprisingly few people on the streets and almost no traffic to remember. Near the city centre was a large music store with at least two floors stuffed with the latest 'state-of-the-art' 1953 television sets and, as far as I knew, like all shops in the city it was closed and firmly secured. However, the morning developed and became very very quiet, until a more senior colleague contacted me. "Have you checked Wilson Pecks store lately?, he asked." "I'm sure I saw a light in there a few minutes ago, we should check it straight away." We checked the building and discovered that the owner had opened the doors for a private viewing of the Coronation to personal friends. They invited us to join them. Here then were two policemen, who, by invitation, saw a great deal of the Coronation, between rainstorms, whilst on duty in Sheffield on that special Bank Holiday.

․ I saw my first TV, a HMV Model 909, in a Brixton shop window in 1937. It was showing cricket. I hated cricket because it was compulsory at my school and I remember thinking that if that was all that television was good for, I, for one, didn't want to have anything to do with it. Wireless was, and still is, my first and only true love. When I first came out of the army I made my living servicing pre-war television sets that some enterprising dealers had mothballed away for seven or eight years, hoping that when the war was over they could make a killing with them. They still worked but often needed a bit of tender loving care to get them going.

My own first set was a kit model that I made myself in 1948. However, I never seemed to get much time to watch it. I later bought a pre-war HMV 900 set for practically nothing and did it up. That was the set that all my family watched the Coronation on. In the weeks leading up to the Coronation you could sell all the sets that you could lay your hands on, no matter how poor the picture quality. On the big day itself I spent all of my time frantically responding to desperate pleas for help from people whose newly- purchased sets had broken down. I must have helped hundreds of people watch history being made but I didn't get a chance to see any of it. After that day, my mates in the repair shop invented a new word - to 'coronate', meaning to run around like a headless chicken. For months afterwards, when one of us was about to lose our temper, we would say 'Look out! He's starting to coronate.'

The HMV shop in London's New Bond St, opened in January, 1938.

IN THE BEGINNING

On 2 November, 1936, the BBC opened the world's first regular television service from Alexandra Palace in North London. The range of the transmitter was only about thirty-five miles and, until the end of 1938, there was only a single studio. Pictures could not be recorded and all programmes had to be transmitted 'live'. Output was modest - about one hour in the afternoon and one and a half hours each evening. There was no transmission at all on Sundays. The number of viewers was extremely small. A year after opening only about two thousand sets had been sold. Sales increased as cheaper models were introduced so that by the Summer of 1939 about twenty thousand televisions were in use. This was still, however, only about one for every six hundred people that could receive pictures.

❧ When the Queen came to Halifax, Nova Scotia, we saw the crowds begin to gather, but decided to go home and watch it on television. Why see the real thing when cameramen with scaffolding and state-of-the-art equipment can do the hard work for you? And why switch on to see your Queen at all? The television doesn't give the true picture. We know your Royal Family are a sort of crazy people, real nuts, but that comes from the Boulevard press, not from television. TV is too respectful.

❧ I was in England the year the Queen was fed up with the whole lot of them - Fergie, Andrew, Di and Charles - and made her Annus Horribilis speech. My gran, mom's mom, was really upset and said that it was a shame. She didn't deserve it and, in any case, she was beautiful. I think that she must have been watching her on the radio or, should I say, wireless. I saw a slightly overweight little old lady.

❧ Quite the most memorable and interesting assignment was when I went to Buckingham Palace to service a television set in a private room. The set was in the corner of the room and there was a chair on each side of it. I had been working on it from the back for a while when in bounced Prince Charles and Princess Anne. I suppose Charles was about ten years old as he was still wearing shorts. Anne had a very sweet smile. Seeing me, they jumped up on the chairs and showed great interest in what I was doing. To deal with the trouble I held a mirror in front of the set so that I could see the picture while making internal adjustments. Charles was intrigued with the mirror idea and asked what it was for. On explaining, he said 'Isn't that clever?'

Watching the 1952 Cup Final at Featherstone Miners' Welfare Hall.

❧ "And don't make any plans for Saturday!", shouted Mom from the bedroom where she was rifling through the sock drawer trying to find me a pair without holes. "We're going to a wedding." My heart sank. I was eleven years old and the only important thing in my life was football. We had already had a bout of Cup Final mania in Sheffield that year, as Wednesday had been to Wembley in May, and, although my loyalties lay on the other side of town, I had wept as openly as everyone else as I watched them get beat by the odd goal in five.

"Yes, it's definitely this Saturday", she said after a small pause, "Three o'clock". Oh no, not three o'clock! Anything but three o'clock. There should be a law against getting married on World Cup Final Day, especially as it is in England, especially as England are playing, and, most especially, at three o'clock.

As we filed out of church after the ceremony and began the three hundred yard walk to the Parson Cross Hotel for the reception, I noticed that some of the men, including the Bridegroom and the Bride's Dad, were running. Caught up in the atmosphere, I too broke into a trot and was one of the first to arrive at the pub. As we entered the concert room, in which the tables were laid out to seat about thirty-five diners, I caught sight of the reason for all the haste. There in the corner, on a rickety old trestle table, was a telly!

I'll never forget how the moods swung that day. From elation to dejection and back again. The sight of fifteen grown men jumping up and down as Geoff Hurst's third goal - and England's fourth, lifted the back of the net, to the accompaniment of Kenneth Wolstenholme shouting, "It is now!". Then came flickering black and white images of footballers in red shirts, celebrating as they ran round the pitch displaying the trophy to all and sundry. Bobby Charlton crying, his brother, Jack, grinning. Alan Ball's squeaky voice interviews and little Nobby Stiles with his funny dance and his front teeth missing.

How the following few hours flew by in a haze of happiness, with my Mom making sure that I didn't have too many sips of beer from the grown-up's glasses.

Whenever that glorious moment is relived on TV, I can still see the small black and white portable telly, with a group of grown men in suits and buttonholes watching the greatest moment in English football, and, across the room, a complementary number of wives and girlfriends, trying their hardest to put on a brave face and wondering whose idea it was to have a wedding on World Cup Final Day.

❧ Thinking back on it, my Mum had a really easy time of it when it came to my birthday parties. My birthday is in the middle of May. Like most little boys I was very keen on football as, of course, were all of my friends. My birthday party was always arranged to be held on the nearest Saturday which also, conveniently, happened to be the day of the FA Cup final. Not for me the joys of pass the parcel or pin the tail on the donkey. No magicians or 'Bobbo the Clown'. We all just sat, glued to the box, jelly and blancmange balanced on our laps, for the duration of the match, before running outside to recreate the match in the street.

❧ I got married when I was eighteen. The war was over and that's what girls did in 1947. He was a good husband as far as providing was concerned. He tipped up and was more generous than most. His father had been a bit of a sod, so his mother was more supportive than most, especially after our Laura came along. Some women give support to their daughters-in-law; Nan was one of those. Three years into the marriage and carrying young Michael I was getting depressed. The bloom of the new council house was wearing a bit thin and I had all the things I had dreamed of - a new settee, a hoover, a spin-dryer and a pantry full of tinned fruit. We had a picture over the hob of a crying girl. Many's the day I knew how she felt.

At first I did all the things that a good wife was supposed to do. I decorated the bedrooms, I baked jam tarts and topped and tailed the upstairs rooms every Wednesday. This wasn't the age when you donkey-stoned the front step and dolly-blued the whites, and so, because I was well organised, I had a lot of time on my hands. Yet I wasn't complaining. Life was getting easier and labour-saving devices were to be had on demand.

Ernie was often on nights and this made for difficulties. But even when he was able to take me out, he wouldn't.

He liked to go out with his mates and the best he could offer was a night at the 'Ivanhoe'. Even there he was restless. He had little conversation and whenever a chance arose he was at the dartboard or playing that skittle game. In the end I got more and more depressed. I found it hard to let him touch me. Eventually, he didn't seem to want to any more. "Pull yourself together", he would say, but never said exactly how. I stopped trying to make myself attractive and got myself put on tablets for my nerves. I was twenty six.

Then one day he came into the kitchen all smiles - he didn't smile a lot in those days, and said something that's rung through my head ever since. "Susan", he said, "Today I have bought you something that will sort out all your problems - a Marconi television".

❧ Before the Second World War my father, who was listening to a programme on the wireless, laughingly remarked, "Wouldn't it be great if there were pictures of this?". Later, at an agricultural show, a closed circuit picture was shown in a tent of the cattle in the showground, where my father was showing a prize cow. However, it was not until after the war that I saw a black and white TV set. But I can't remember if my father ever saw one. Sadly, I don't think he did.

❧ In the early 1930s I sat in front of a wooden box about four feet square to watch TV. You might think that strange if you believe that television wasn't operational then. At the time, I was employed in a Barnsley radio store and the box in front of me had aroused a great amount of interest, being something out of the normal.

The box was about five inches deep and enclosed a disc two and a half feet in diameter which was driven by an electric motor. The disc had a series of holes drilled in a concentric circle. In the front of the box, near the top, was a window with a lens and at the rear of the disc was a neon lamp. As the disc revolved a rectangular pattern of light appeared on the lens approximately one and one half inches deep by one inch across. When a signal was transmitted from an early television station the intensity of the neon light varied from full brilliance to off. A pulse was transmitted to ensure that the speed of the motor was kept in sympathy with the signal transmitted. The picture viewed when looking into the lens was not always satisfactory. Signals transmitted were limited to a head and shoulders image of a man or woman accompanied by the sound of the news or a song. Although today it could only be considered a very elementary transmission of sight, nevertheless it was a momentous achievement.

My second memory of TV was in 1936, when, as a member of a party to Crystal Palace, I was invited to a large house in Sydenham, South London to watch a demonstration of a television system developed by J L Baird and sponsored by the Bush Radio Company. Crystal Palace was being used as a transmitting station whilst the pictures were being received in the house in Sydenham. The picture of hundreds of sea birds flying off the cliffs of South England has always remained in my memory.

About this time the British Broadcasting Corporation were considering an experimental television programme and the Baird Company and the EMI were in competition for the contract. Unfortunately for J L Baird, the contract was awarded to EMI and the system accepted is basically the same today.

*Viewing experimental broadcasts in 1930 on a Baird 'Televisor'.
John Logie Baird is standing in the centre of the group.*

Televising the Boat Race in 1949.

In 1933, when I was just three years old, we moved to a newly-built housing development at Petts Wood, near Orpington in Kent. We lived in a 'private' cul-de-sac called the Chenies (I never found out the origin of the name). My father was a metallurgist working for J Stone and Co, manufacturers of bronze ships' propellers and light-alloy aircraft parts, at their factory in Deptford. Our neighbours were mostly businessmen. I remember Mr Pearce, proprietor of Pearce Signs and Mr Christlieb, accountant to J Arthur Rank. Our immediate neighbour on one side was Mr Nicholls and his family. He was a director of the Maconochie food company. All the residents of the road of some thirty detached, 1930s half-timbered, houses were obviously affluent.

One sunny afternnon we children were called in to see the boat race on the Nicholl's television set. I remember it as a dark polished wooden cabinet sitting on the floor of their lounge. It was about three feet high, about the same in length and about a foot deep. The screen was tiny - perhaps five or six inches wide. The picture was bright but I cannot remember how clear it was. In fact it was very difficult to see anything at all because of all the people crowded around it. I was not particularly interested in rowing, so I can't remember who won the race.

🔸 I saw my first television in 1937 and you cannot be a much earlier viewer than that. I was working for the London Co-operative at the time and I had delivered something to a house in Teddington. There was this big box in the corner of theroom with a flickering picture coming from it. My first reaction was that I didn't think much of it and, although I wasn't one of the sort that said that it would never go anywhere, I thought that it wasn't a patch on the cinema.

When I came back after the war, television had moved on a bit and, although it was still confined to the London area, it had improved technically by leaps and bounds. The programmes were still bland, usually studio productions. The outdoor potential of television was recognised, but was fraught with difficulty. The programmes constantly broke down and when they did, a test card or, more likely, a short called "The Interlude" appeared. Such was the success of these pieces that people had views about their worth. By popular concensus, the one which showed swans on a river was less exciting than the view of a potter's hands throwing a cylinder. A kitten playing with a ball of wool was also very popular.

Joan Miller and friends admiring a HMV set, 1937.

Watching a GEC television, December 1936.

*Rehearsals for post-war television,
the Windmill Girls in front of the camera, April, 1946.*

TV AND WORLD WAR TWO
On 1 September, 1939, two days before the outbreak of the Second World War, BBC television was closed down. No announcement was made. The oficial reason was that the transmissions would have acted as a beacon, guiding German bombers to their targets in London. At midday a Mickey Mouse cartoon was shown. When it ended the screen went blank. Screens were to remain blank for nearly seven years. Television did not begin again until 7 June, 1946 with the pre-war announcer, Jasmine Bligh, saying 'Remember me?'

❧ I saw a television set depicted in a brand new encyclopedia I received one Christmas morning. In the "scientific discoveries" section, sat a very young, smiling, Sylvia Peters, surrounded by some sort of box. I wasn't very old at the time and the words 'television', and 'Alexandra Palace' were a bit big to get my tongue round, so I said to the fount of all wisdom, my father, "What is it?". "It's a special box", he said, "that receives pictures transmitted through the air, like the wireless waves we pick up with that big pole at the bottom of the garden." He's mad, I thought. You can't have pictures zooming through the air like that. "I've seen one working", said Dad, who was manager of the local Co-op and got down to London on occasional buying trips. "Why haven't we got them in Scunthorpe Dad?" "Because the signal isn't strong enough to reach here yet", he replied. "It'll only be a year or two and then we'll have one." The war intervened. No television!

❧ My wife and I were courting. We went with her parents, in their car, one evening - it must have been 1952 - to see the Blackpool Illuminations. We drove up the prom, South to North, viewing the lights from the car. When we came to the end of the Golden Mile we turned right and stopped to buy fish and chips at a shop in a parade. One of the nearby shops sold televisions and, although it was late evening, a set had been left on in the shop window.

We watched fascinated. That whetted my future father-in-law's desire to own a set. Within a few weeks he had bought a 12" Pye console set which we all thought was marvellous.

One particular thing which sticks in my memory is that if anything at all 'suggestive' - and in those early days 'suggestive' might be a couple kissing! - was shown, he would lean forward and switch the set off!

❧ My father, who died a month ago, aged 91, was a pioneer of early television. Long before the Second World War, I believe signals were transmitted from the roof of Selfridges in London. When my father wrote and told them he had got reception in Hull, they were very surprised it had reached as far as Yorkshire. I remember seeing a photograph of my father standing beside this TV. It was very different from today's models, being a wheel spun at so many revs a minute. The picture was postcard size.

I was born in 1939 and one of my earliest memories is the smell of solder as Dad was busy making yet another TV with a 9" screen. I was eight years old when I saw my first television picture. It was a young girl playing the piano. We were probably the very first people in Hull to have television.

❧ Our first television was a little Bush and it was back in 1953. We were one of the first in our street in Keighley to get a television, but I never had much happiness watching it. The only reason that we could afford it was because I was pregnant and had been saving up to buy a pram. The baby was still-born and we used the pram money to buy the television. It still upsets me to think of it now. Happily, I had a baby the following year.

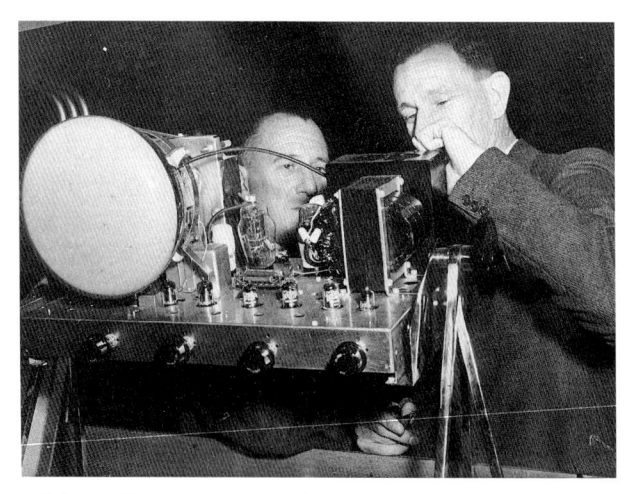

Radiolympia Show, 1947. Discussing the merits of an 'Ekco' Television.

*One of the exhibits at the Television Exhibition,
held at the Science Museum in 1933.*

🌿 My father, Charles Henry Wood, was a miner and had no training whatsoever in electrics. We were the first family on our street to have a television set. My father made it himself. It was like magic to us kids. The neighbours were amazed as well. I have to laugh when I think about that television because when my father made the cabinet and put the picture-tube into it, nothing happened. Like many of his DIY projects, it just wouldn't work. The valves would only work when they were outside the set. So all the innards sat on top of the cabinet while we watched 'Bewitched' and 'Take Your Pick'.

The Radio Show, Earls Court, 1953.
Television display on the Ultra radio stand.

A Cossor television set, 1937.

I was ten years old when television first entered my home in 1957. We were intrigued with this new piece of furniture which now resided in the corner of the front room. It didn't look like a TV of today - it was a piece of furniture; a walnut cabinet with mahogany trim. It had two doors which opened from the middle, and no glass in sight. The screen was made of material silk, - I think, which displayed one channel - BBC.

When Scottish television arrived it was known as Channel 10 - the catchphrase was "Hey, Hey - It's Channel 10" - but the walnut cabinet had no facility to be tuned to this new station. My husband was a TV engineer apprentice and one of his jobs was to convert this type of set. He drilled four holes on the side of the cabinet which allowed the tuner unit for receiving the new station to be mounted. The favourite programme of the day was "The One O'Clock Gang" with Larry Marshall, which ran for many years. The first soap broadcast in Scotland on the BBC was "The Grove family", broadcast live once a week.

When BBC2 was introduced to Scotland, our piece of furniture became no more than just that. It was converted into a linen cabinet and still stands in my mother's home today.

❧ In 1947 I acquired a pre-war combined Marconiphone all-wave radio and television set which had been sold originally to someone in the Alexandra Palace area. As I had been a radio service engineer most of my life, I repaired this receiver and managed to get a picture on the 5" cathode ray tube. I erected a forty-foot-high mast at the side of our bungalow and occasionally received poor pictures from the, now re-established Alexandra Palace transmitter.

In those days TV was limited to two hours each evening and weekdays - two afternoon one-hour sessions for women and an hour-long session on Sundays for children. When, a few years later, the BBC opened its new transmitter at Sutton Coldfield to cover the Midlands area, I received very good pictures, partly because we lived about four hundred feet above sea level. I was the first person in Swansea to have a TV licence, which, in those days, cost £2. The post office staff were in turmoil, not having received such a request previously. Receiving pictures was, of course, a wonder to people who didn't have TV. As you can imagine, they came to my house in droves.

Shortly after this, some enterprising dealers in the area picked places where there was fair reception to sell their sets. I helped quite a few people to get a decent picture.

THE SPREAD OF TELEVISION

Until 1949 there was just one transmitter, Alexandra Palace, and television could only be enjoyed by people in the London area. In December, 1949 a second transmitter was opened at Sutton Coldfield to serve the Midlands. Holme Moss, for the North followed in 1951, then Kirk o'Shotts for Scotland in 1952 together with Wenvoe for the West Country. Eighty per cent of the population could now receive television.

When ITV began in 1955, it too began transmitting in London only. Unlike the BBC, however, it was to spread rapidly. By 1956 ITV covered the Midlands and the North and, by 1957, Central Scotland as well. The following year saw coverage expand to South Wales and the West of England. Before the end of the decade, ITV could be received in Northern Ireland, the North East and East Anglia.

The television showroom at Christopher Pratt's, Bradford in about 1955.

❧ It was the talk of our street back in the December of '49. A strange 'H' shaped device had suddenly appeared on the top of our chimney. Not only did it look like a tuning fork, but it sometimes sounded like one too when the winter winds blew across the hill on which our bungalow stood.

Saturday brought a crowd of curious neighbours round to see the latest wonder - a television. Concealed in a smart walnut cabinet, you opened two doors to reveal a massive 12" screen. Two large knobs controlled brightness and volume, while nineteen valves glowed in the back like a minature Blackpool Illuminations.

I can still remember that first night as we waited for the programme to start. Children's TV ran from 5.00 until 6.00 pm and the adult programmes from 7.00 until 9.00 pm. In between shows a leisurely windmill turned or an industrious potter entertained us. Finally, the main programme began with a pantomime from Wembley Stadium - "Red Riding Hood on Ice". Amazed, we watched the monochrome picture as the fixed camera caught glimpses of the skating figures. A commentator talked constantly explaining what it was we were seeing. It was as if he still thought he was on radio.

Later that week came the comedy shows. "Folly Mill" with its 'laughing fiddle' theme. As far as I can remember, a family had won the pools, bought an old mill and started a farm. Next was the "Birds and the Bees" - two couples living next door in a high-rise flat. Crime was headed by "Fabian of the Yard", while fictional detectives were headed by "Mark Saber". Children were entertained by "Larry the Lamb" and "Tramp Toadstool". Puppet type shows were very popular then, with "Muffin the Mule" being king of them all. Wonderful Robert Harbin performed magic, like levitating tables and pushing glass cubes through a female assistant chained in a open box. He also had his own children's adventure series in which a statue in a square mysteriously loses its head.

"Cafe Continental" brought in stars from all over Europe. Do you remember the "Mad Professor" act in which a small man controlled a Frankenstein monster from a control panel? At the end of the act the monster pulled the professor to pieces to show he was a dummy. Then the monster took off his mask and showed he was a man. Years later I saw the very same act in the Tivoli Gardens Cafe in Denmark.

Today, television seems very commonplace and sadly lacks the magic of those first basic, yet enthralling, TV shows.

❧ It was in the dark, dreary days before cable TV and video recorders that I first began to take an interest in British television. Living in Rhode Island, USA, my only access to programmes came via the local PBS (Public Broadcast System) station, coming out of Boston. Unfortunately, the signal was very poor and it was only through utilising the greatest creative thought that it was possible to make any sense whatsoever of the static and snow on the screen. the 'best' picture (ie the one where you could actually make out shapes and hear some dialogue) could be achieved only by going up into the attic with a small, black and white portable. Using coat hangers, assorted cutlery and yards of aluminium foil it was possible to receive a palatable picture, provided you dimmed the lights and squinted from across the room. This was how I watched "Dr Who", Monday through Friday at 7.30pm. My mother, of course, scolded me that I would ruin my eyes or my brain or something. She never could understand what I found so appealing about a children's show I couldn't even see properly! Her anger escalated when I diversified into watching "Monty Python" which she deemed too risque for a ten year old. Still, she never actually forbade me from watching anything, though she would lecture me incessantly afterwards. I also discovered such comedy classics as "No Honestly", "The Rise and Fall of Reginald Perrin", "The Good Life" and "Fawlty Towers". Today, I can see most of those shows and countless others with the perfect reception of cable and the choice of nearly fifty channels. VCRs allow me the luxury of 'time shifting' and the ability to view the same little skit over and over again. Still, I fondly remember sweltering in the Summer heat of the old attic, hoping that the inevitable thunderstorm would hold off just long enough for me to catch the Tardis taking off to another adventure.

The old and the new.
Television aerial on a Gloucestershire thatched cottage, 1953.

☙ Shortly after the war, test transmissions from Ally-Pally started again. The Co-op in our town was a very tall building and the electricians rigged up aerials on the roof. The great day came when they were going to attempt to receive the transmission. As I remember, it was in the evening and I was allowed to stay up with Dad to see it. What a disappointment! Shadowy figures, squiggles and interference. Where was the beautiful Sylvia Peters? Surely it had to be better than this.? Soon it was. We stuck with it and well before the Coronation we were the proud possessors of a Defiant Console model with a very small 9" screen. Those early television sets must have caused ructions in lots of households as the proud owners desperately tried to tune them in. "Is it bright enough? - "No!" - "Is it now?" - "No!" - "It's got to be. You can't be looking at it right".

☙ It was 1950 when television arrived in our home. Mother bought a friend's old one as she was buying a newer model. Our secondhand Marconi was installed in a corner of the front room - well, one couldn't have this wonderful new invention in one's living kitchen. The piano we all played stood closed and silent in the opposite corner. The entire room was re-arranged and chairs were placed fan-like facing the huge mahogany cabinet. Then, mother moved my father around the room. She did this because she said it helped reception. Father was always in trouble with my mum for walking passed our old wireless and making it oscillate. Finally she decided where he should sit and then began to rearrange the rest of the family.

One day, mother came in from shopping to find my eighty-four year old grandfather and four of his elderly friends sprawled around our living room, the air thick with their cigarette and pipe smoke. They were all engrossed in the new children's programme on television. Mother turned off the set and sent the four old gentlemen home, saying that the smoke was getting into the set and damaging it.

Smoke gets in your eyes.
Television viewing 1970.

❧ When I was about eleven years old I remember that a neighbour in our street got a TV set. Most of my friends had come from the same background as myself - a large family and not a lot of money, living in a council house. We all used to stand in the street by the front gate, looking over the wall at the set in their front room. A few months later, my parents rented a set of our own. We were fascinated. For the first few weeks my Mum used to rearrange all the furniture before we watched. We were eight children. My brother was doing his National Service. When he came home on leave the house must have looked like a cinema. The chairs were arranged in rows, the lights were off and mum had made us toffee apples. We all sat there goggle-eyed. It was great. I'll never forget the saturday when our TV was delivered.

❧ Unfortunately, as our industrial village was in a valley, the signal strength was very low and, as electrical suppressors were not in general use, it would not be too long before the screen was rendered hideous by screeches and jagged bands that ran horizontally across across the surface. When this happened, Ada, who as the dominant partner took charge of such matters, would grab a broom and storm out along the terrace of houses, knocking at each window and shouting, "Who's got a vacuum on then?"

It was inevitable that others would buy or rent television sets. But when her next door neighbour, Herbert, acquired one, Ada was convinced that the aerial was affecting her signal and so she raised her aerial another few feet. Herbert took umbrage at this and the next day his aerial was at the same level. And so the great aerial race began. Soon both aerials were waving like tall poplars in the breeze. It was difficult to see where the rivalry would end. We arrived one day to be greeted by Ada exulting over the latest move. When we looked at the roof we saw what appeared to be an iron bedstead fixed at a dizzy height above the chimney. Upon closer inspection this turned out to be two aerials bolted together a few feet apart, swaying perilously. Unfortunately a high wind had been forecast. When it arrived the whole contraption disintegrated and rods, nuts, bolts and wires descended with a clatter into the street.

Luckily, an enterprising firm was now in the process of erecting a master aerial on top of a nearby hill and offering villagers the opportunity of connecting to it for a small fee. As we were in a worse state than Ada, being in the lee of the hill, we jumped at the chance, bought a television set and settled down to a near perfect picture. But in some senses it was never the same and we took pleasure in harking back to the spectacle of a puce-faced Ada rushing along her street shouting, "Who's got a vacuum on then?"

WHAT'S IN A NAME?
'The BBC has adopted the word 'Televiewer' to indicate those who look at televised pictures. By international agreement amongst scientific societies the suffix 'or' indicates an instrument, and therefore we have 'Televiewor' to indicate the apparatus used for viewing television. The verb 'to Televise' is already in use for the act of sending out or transmitting television, and 'to Teleview' seems indicated as the obvious verb for the act of using a Televiewor.'
From *Televiewing* by Ernest H Robinson, 1937.

People who listened to the wireless were *listeners* but what should people who watch television be called? A number of different names were suggested, including *lookers, gazers, watchers, visionists, witnessers* and *teleseers* before *viewer* became accepted as the norm.

The slang term *couch potato* has recently become popular. The origins of this phrase are somewhat tenuous. *Couch* is clear enough, but why *potato*? The reasoning is as follows. A potato is a sort of tuber. By extension, a tuber is also someone who watches a tube, as in Cathode Ray Tube - hence, *couch potato*.

Members of the Lancing Televiewers Club,
using their homemade apparatus to detect sources of interference, 1949.

☙ We lived in the village of Uppermill, Saddleworth - o'er top, as they say here. The transmitter was at Belmont. Therefore, reception was very poor, due in part to the hills. To get a decent picture often meant wandering round the house with the aerial held out and finding a place to put it. The children didn't seem to mind when each Saturday those who lived close to us congregated in my sitting room to watch Jim Dale and Josephine Douglass present "The Six Five Special". There were so many shadows on the screen, even the solo performers looked like a group.

We were discussing the poor reception one day at the woollen mill where I worked evenings, when one of the women, Nancy, said, "We can't get a picture at all, but they can next door and so we sling the wire through the window and use their aerial. The only drawback is that they have it fixed to the foot of their bed. He works shifts and there are times when we can't tell whether our picture is doing a rhumba or a samba, especially on a Sunday afternoon when they have a matinee!"

In those days we had such wonderful programmes: Tim Fraser in the Francis Durbridge series, looking all sexy in his sheepskin coat leaning on his slinky sports car, "Tonight" with Cliff Michelmore. Maybe it was because television was new, but as far as I am concerned, the quality was much better than it is today. More entertaining.

☙ In the late 40s the only place where you could get television round here was Beacon Hill in Bradford. My uncle lived close by and got one in 1947. There were only about three others I knew of at that time. It had a 9" screen with a 4" magnifier and you had to look at it dead on or it was all distorted. Televisions used to break down all the time - not the sets, but the programmes. The card would come on - it was a fancy card with scrolled edges that said, "Back soon" - and we'd sit there time after time with a cup of tea watching the card until the programme came back on.

☙ A very old lady lived next door to us who had an old 17-inch TV, black and white, which she used to cover at night with an old cloth, because she thought it gave it a better 'film' the next day. She would also do this if one of the announcers had a cold so she didn't catch it. When they brought out the first colour programmes, she invited half her family to watch on her black and white set. Someone had told her she only had to move her indoor aerial sideways to get a colour picture.. She sat all evening with her family, but nobody saw any colours except her. "Look, he's got a blue shirt on." When she did realise her telly didn't get colour, she blamed the BBC for rationing the colour.

☙ In the mid 1950s, the YMCA in Castleford obtained its first television. It all began when a furniture company rented the large downstairs room to house an exhibition. Three-piece suites, coffee tables and the inevitable oak standard lamps were arranged tastefully around a television set. During the day, the exhibition was open to the public - the television being an added attraction. After 10.00pm each weekday night it became my miracle box. The steward and his wife had obtained permission to switch the television set on and watch the programmes for the last hour before locking up for the night. For one whole week, six of us settled down in the plush easy chairs and watched the Edinburgh Tattoo. It was magic. None of us possessed a TV set. An idea grew. As the furniture company prepared to move out, we remembered a little-used room on the top floor. This was the start of our dream and it did not take long before we had sold our dream to most of the other members.

The YMCA was used to the idea of team work. Dominoes, table tennis, billiards and many more activities all revolved around the word 'team'. Here was something completely different - TV. No silver cups to play for or medals to be won. Simple, effortless entertainment at the flick of a switch. We mentioned our idea to the manager of the furniture company and he gave us a roll of lino. The TV set went back to the shop it came from but not before we had obtained a promise that we could buy it at cost. 'Cost' became our battle cry. We held jumble sales and whist drives, papered and painted the room and put down the new lino. We bought the TV set and I became engaged to the only single Tattoo watcher. Almost every time I went upstairs to watch the set it was switched on to a boxing or football match. Downstairs, the teams were still busy - dominoes, table tennis and billiards. Now, years later, I cherish my husband's billiards cups and table tennis medals, remember with joy the Edinburgh Tattoo and get to choose my own television programmes.

♣ Kids in school playgrounds everywhere have always, and will always, indulge in bragging matches. When I was at school in the early 1960s and all the mileage had gone from simply owning a television, one of my classmates came up with the ultimate brag. "Well, we've got a gas television, so there!" They were always in advance of everybody else. I remember the first family in our street to get a car. It was a maroon-coloured Morris Minor. They were also the first family in the street to get a television - black and white of course!

♣ Our dad always wanted to be the first with everything in our street. He was one of the first to have a television. He was the first to have a patio - he built it himself by planting hundreds of old red house bricks on end. He was the first to 'flush' all the doors in the house and, in later years, the first to strip the flushing off again to reveal the original pine. He certainly had that icon of 1970s culture - the Hitachi music centre, before anyone else. But his greatest claim was that he was the first man able to receive BBC 2 television transmissions in our neck of the woods. Never mind the snowy reception. Never mind the fact that it showed mostly documentaries and he didn't have a blind bit of interest in them. Never mind that two-thirds of the year he worked nights. He had BBC 2. What's more he had the aerial to prove it. It looked different to other people's aerials and so our house stood out from the rest in the terraced row. Not that it didn't already - our dad was also the first to have hanging baskets, a bird box, and if you pressed the doorbell it played "The Entrance of the Gladiators". Many's the time I've seen dad standing proudly in the street looking up and telling anybody who could be bothered to listen, "That aerial can pick up BBC 2, you know"

♣ We were one of the few who had one in our area back in 1948. It was a prominent piece of furniture, a 12" screen in a large case. I couldn't wait to get home from work on the day it was delivered. Ours was a small room so we were sitting quite close to the screen. Mother switched on and the picture started to roll very slowly. I said it would probably stop, but it didn't, so we thought our eyes must have to adjust to the rolling. This went on for two days and by this time we were feeling quite sick. My brother came on his weekly visit and twiddled a knob at the back of the set, making the picture stable. We couldn't believe we had sat for two days looking at a rolling picture. Was I relieved.

♣ Many years in the television sales and repair business have convinced me that there is an unwritten rule that applies to all sets - a sort of Baird's Law, so to speak. Baird's Law states that the size of a television set is inversely proportional to the size of the room that it is in. In other words, the smaller the house, the bigger the telly.

I once had to deliver a huge 21" English Electric set to a tiny, two-up, two-down gravedigger's cottage. The set was too big to go through the front door and, in the end, we had to take out the front window to get it in. The people in the house could not sit far enough away from the screen so as not to see the lines on the picture. I had told them that they didn't need such a big set but they wouldn't listen.

On the other hand, I was once called to fix the set belonging to local JP who lived in an enormous house - practically a mansion. He only had a 9" Baird portable that he kept in a cupboard. Not liking clutter, he would only bring it out on the very rare occasions that he wanted to view.

The largest set in the 1951 Radio Show - A HMV model 1903.

A Sony transistorised TV set - The smallest set in the world, 1964.

About ten years ago I was working for the Comet service department. It was Christmas Eve and I was rushing around in a vain attempt to deliver repaired TVs in time for Christmas. One delivery took me to a block of flats. The customer lived on the thirteenth floor and the lift was out of order. As the set was very heavy I tried to get as close to the entrance to the flats as possible. I drove my van across a grassy area in front of the flats but ground to a halt about twenty yards short. My Ford Transit had sunk up to its axles in mud. For nearly an hour I tried to get out. The grassed area had by this time turned into what looked like a ploughed field.

I called for help and decided to take the TV set up while I was waiting.

After struggling up thirteen flights of stairs, I managed to ring the doorbell with my elbow. My arms were like lead weights and I had lost all sense of feeling in my fingers. Just as the customer opened the door, I dropped the set. One angry customer - no TV for Christmas! I carried the pieces of the set all the way back down to my van, only to find someone from the council waiting for me, who told me that I was being reported.

A few months later I was summoned to court, charged with criminal damage to the grass. I was lucky. The case was dismissed since the council's expert did not visit the scene until two weeks after the event. The magistrate felt that, in that case, the damage could have been caused at any time from Christmas Eve onwards.

The TV repair shop at Christopher Pratt's, Bradford, 1960.

☙ The first TV repair men weren't really used to televisions. They had gained all their practical experience with wireless sets. Rather than spend time investigating the real cause of a fault, many of them would simply announce 'The tube has gone'. We had a simple formula for working out the cost of a new tube - £1 per inch, plus purchase tax, plus fitting cost. Most of the time there was nothing wrong with the tube at all - the fault was elsewhere. In our repair shop we used to repair, on average, seventy sets each week. I doubt if we had to replace more than twelve tubes a year and most of those, I suspect, were broken in the back of the van when the sets were being brought in for repair.

☙ The Knottingley caller was a 'pain in the butt'. His television had blacked out, but instead of courteously asking if I would call round it was 'Get round here immediately if you know what's good for you.' Friday passed without my having any intention of going. Saturday brought the second abusive call and I promised to be there before the end of the afternoon. However, I still had no intention of going. He couldn't get at me on Sunday and, by Monday I detected a slight change of tone in his voice. I decided that if he continued to be a little more respectful, I would probably make it by Thursday morning. The house was a tip - old clothes, chip paper and bits of motorcycle everywhere. Sitting in a chair in the middle of the room was a dull-eyed little man with a Tetley beer belly. The house stank. Since he had had no stimulation of any kind for almost a week, he was slightly comatose. 'It just went blank', he said. I moved the settee to get at the back of the set. I did not need my screwdriver. There, stiff as a board, lay his pet alsatian who had foolishly decided to chew through the power cable.

☙ As a young apprentice I remember calling to visit a woman who had been experiencing terrible smells in her house. In her desperation she had even called in the council to inspect her drains but they could find nothing wrong. The real reason for the smell only became apparent when her television broke down. In those days, her Bush television used a selenium rectifier. Just before these failed, they could give off a pungent smell for weeks. The sort of smell that got you looking at the soles of your shoes in case you had stepped in something on the way in.

☙ It's ironic really, considering that I've been involved in selling and repairing televisions for most of my working life, but I can't stand watching TV. I'm an active sort of person and like to keep on the go. Television is far too constricting. I much prefer to listen to records or the radio. The only time that I sit and watch television for any length of time is at Christmas when I go to stay with my sister. I invariably fall asleep.

☙ Our first set was a table-top Philips model which incorporated a world radio waveband across the top and a 9" screen on one side. The aerial consisted of a long wire from the roof down the length of our long garden and, to us, the reception was perfect. Of course there was no choice of channels - BBC London only, so as 'exiled' Londoners living on a farm in South Bedfordshire - my husband was a returned POW who could not face the pace of city life again - it made me feel less isolated and away from civilisation. I realise now what an extravagant purchase it must have been. The price of the set equalled about twenty weeks of the salary that my husband was then earning as a farm secretary.

Viewing time was very limited; "Picture Page" with Sylvia Peters some afternoons seemed to be a rehearsal for its showing again in the evening when the programmes lasted, I think, from about 8.30 to 10.00 pm. There were no news bulletins in those days. TV sets were so rare that some 'locals' would come to our cottage asking to see this new marvel, even when no programmes were showing, just for the thrill of seeing the screen light up or to watch the test card. When "Muffin the Mule" and "Andy Pandy" were first shown I had to send in reports to the BBC on the reactions of my two young daughters. My son was born three weeks after we bought our TV set, so I spent many happy hours watching the 1948 Olympic Games taking place in London, while nursing him.

Sylvia Peters pictured in 1955.

❧ Sylvia Peters was the first person I remember seeing on television and then Mary McKenzie. Both very beautiful to look at and beautifully spoken too. Then there was Annette Mills with "Muffin the Mule". We watched everything. My favourite programme was Eric Robinson with "Music For You"; Shirley Bassey made her TV debut on his programme, singing a song not at all like the ones she belts out now. Another favourite was "Animal, Vegetable, Mineral" with Mortimer Wheeler, Hugh David and Dr Bronowski. How I envied their knowledge.

There was nothing like TV in those days and I remember ours cost £100, a lot of money then. But, for all that, it didn't broadcast twenty-four hours a day, thank goodness. We still sat at table for our meals.

❧ My Uncle Eric was an all Black Country Staffordshire male, who worked on a lathe at Averys, cleaned his shoes nightly and read the Westerns of Zane Grey. In no sense did he have a questioning mind. To that extent he was not much different from the rest of the homophobic, racist, sexist West Bromwich Albion supporters who lived at the Margaret Gardens end of our council estate. Except he once made a remark about television which has stuck with me for the last forty years. I would be about seventeen and, having heard that Dylan Thomas died of a surfeit of loose women and whisky, was becoming interested in the arts for the best possible reasons. Uncle Eric sensed this and so on one of my weekly visits sought to confide that he was not without redemption by leaning over to me, blacking brush at the ready, and saying, "I saw 'Ballet for Beginners' on the set last night. You know, I think that it's got something to it has ballet."
Shortly afterwards ITV came along.

❧ Nobody believes this, but it is true. We had a colour television in 1957. Dad had purchased from someone a piece of plastic which fitted across the front of the set. At the top it was blue. As your eye travelled downwards, the blue merged to pink and at the bottom it was green. Well, think about it. The sky is blue, we are pink and the grass is green. It was alright in a surreal sort of way. In close up, Cliff Michelmore looked like the 'Last of the Mohicans' in heavy warpaint.

❧ When Yorkshire TV announced, "Colour is coming your way", father could hardly contain himself. He couldn't wait to see the horse racing in colour and went into an ecstasy of expectation at the thought of the 'Minstrels' in colour. When the big day came, he was furious, fit to be tied, promising horrendous and unknown fates to anyone who mentioned colour TV again in his presence.

Being seventy years old and a bit deaf, not to mention being unused to modern technology, he had neither heard nor understood that a new set was required in order to have colour. He thought he could just switch on his black and white and it would be there, especially as it said colour on the screen. From then until he died at seventy-six, anyone who mentioned colour programmes on TV were regaled as "Bloody liars" from deep inside father's armchair.

THE COMING OF COLOUR

Baird had experimented with colour television as early as 1928. It was not until 1955, however, that the BBC began test transmissions in colour. In America, the National Television System Committee (NTSC) had proposed a colour system in 1951. Variable in quality, it earned the nickname 'Never Twice the Same Colour'. Here, matters were complicated by the fact that we were alone in still using the 405 line standard, as introduced in 1936.

The start of BBC2 in 1964, using 625 lines and UHF frequencies meant that a colour system could be agreed and inroduced. On 1 July, 1967, BBC2 screened Wimbledon in colour and became the first colour service in Europe. A critic famously remarked 'Even bad programmes are good in colour'.

The start of colour television. BBC cameras at Wimbledon, July 1967.

❧ "Café Continental" was a favourite and included comics, conjurors and dancers. My most vivid memory was the hostess, Helene Cordet, a French lady and a distant relative of Prince Philip. She had only two evening dresses which she alternated wearing each week.

After "Café Continental" there followed a play, which was always repeated one evening during the week. Sometimes we saw "The Black and White Minstrel Show", singers and dancers with blackened faces. In those days, all the announcers wore evening dress, only showing their top halves. Many comics made jokes about the BBC being unable to afford to buy their announcers a pair of trousers.

❧ We bought our first set in April, 1950, a 9" with four pre-selected radio stations. The first person we saw was Larry Adler, and the most outstanding serial I remember was "The Little Red Monkey". I cannot recall the story, but can still hear the music. At that time my husband's very elderly grandmother was staying with us and she used to 'dress' to watch the news each evening. In those early days newscasters were very elegant in dinner jacket and bow-tie and she thought that she was behaving in an appropriate manner.

❧ We hadn't worked out where you sat or what you sat on to watch television. So, as my mother stood behind us holding the aerial high above her head, dad and me took two dining room chairs and drew them close up to the set. These were the early years and the location of the aerial and the seating arrangements mattered. One friend said that his aerial hung from a nail hammered into a picture frame and that occasionally they picked up the sound on the gas cooker.

In those days the curtains were closed when you watched, but you were told that it was not a good idea to view in total darkness, so a small light shone in the corner. A boyfriend's father reckoned that you could get impotent if you got too close to the set. Maybe, but my experience of his son didn't support the family theory.

❧ Sunday night was bath night and, as usual, my oldest sister sat bathing as the TV played away. I asked whether the people on TV could see us and I was assured by her that they could not see into our home. After a lengthy discussion, I had convinced myself that if we could see them, then they could see us. Then my turn came for the zinc bath on the hearth. I didn't want to undress, as the newsreader was looking in my direction. When I finally got undressed, the newsreader began to laugh for no apparent reason. I grabbed the towel and covered myself up, crying, "He's laughing at me because I have nothing on, and I'm fat". I was certain he could see me and that was the cause of his laughter and I wouldn't venture into the bath until the TV was turned off. From that day on I would never take a bath whilst the TV played.

ARE YOU SITTING COMFORTABLY?
Early viewers were offered helpful advice on how to get the best out of their viewing:

'Viewing in a completely dark room will cause eye strain, which usually results in headaches. Therefore, at night, a low wattage table or wall lamp positioned to avoid light falling directly on the screen should be used. If viewed too closely, the complete structure of the picture will be visible making viewing both difficult and tiring. Generally speaking, the viewing distance for a 10" cathode-ray tube is about 6ft, while for a 15" tube the distance will be be approximately 9ft. Seating arrangements should provide an exit from the room without disturbing other viewers. The picture should be at, or below, eye level so that the viewer will not have to sit looking up at the screen.'

Gathered around the set in 1954.

🍃 We used to sit in darkened rooms with just the firelight flickering - no adverts yet to enable one to nip out to make a cup of tea. Discussions took place next morning at work as to what we thought of the shows. Woe betide you if you had missed Gilbert Harding being rude - and whatever became of that "Sagger Maker's Bottom Knocker" from "What's My Line?"

Watching without Mother, 1951.

> I was initiated into television around forty years ago. I was a night truck driver for Philips Electrical and bought a Consul telly through the company. Programmes those days didn't start until about four in the afternoon. I brought the telly home when I finished my shift and fitted an aerial on the wall by splitting a dual cable and putting one wire vertical and the other horizontal. Then, before retiring to bed, I asked my wife to wake me as soon as the telly came on. At four o'clock I got the call, and dashed downstairs in anticipation, to be greeted by "Andy Pandy" and the "Flower Pot Men" - 'flobber globs' and all. Can you imagine the ear-bashing my loved one came in for. Two hours sleep lost for "Andy Pandy".

> When I was about six years old I used to watch lots of Saturday television and used to love "The Incredible Hulk". Best of all, I loved the part where he changed into the hulk. I would copy him. First, I would make my eyes go white by looking up. Then I would grit my teeth and, there you have it, the transformation complete. I was The Incredibly Small Hulk. I would then throw my bike over the two foot high fence.

> There was one programme on television that I thought was scarier than anything on Earth (well, I thought so anyway) - "Worzel Gummidge"! I don't know why, but as soon as it came on I would go and sit in the kitchen. My big brother knew that I hated it, so he would turn the TV round so that it was facing the kitchen which meant that I would have to run outside to get away from the dreaded worzel. I think what scared me most was his big, pointed nose. Noses really got to me. It wasn't just Worzel Gummidge, it was the wicked witch from the Wizard of Oz and the child catcher from "Chitty Chitty Bang Bang". Anyone with a big nose - except Sgt Cryer from "The Bill" - still makes me feel anxious.

❧ I think that the best programme I ever watched was "The A Team". I watched it every week and nagged my mum to buy me all the toys. The character I liked most was B.A.Baracuss, even though Face, Hannibal and Murdock were cool as well. I loved how B.A. used to knock five guys out with one punch and I liked it when he always said 'sucker'. When me and my friends used to play the a Team we would always fight over who would play B.A. To settle who would have the honour, we would all have to make something useful out of something that was useless, like a gun made out of a toilet roll. Whoever made the best thing was crowned B.A. for the day. I never got to be B.A.

❧ In September 1966, my husband and I moved to Boston to run a public house. The locals welcomed us, but sarcastically added that they were pleased we weren't there when the World Cup was on, because the public bar didn't have a television set. My husband retorted that he hadn't had time to buy one yet. By the time we eventually got a TV for the bar, I was being excused duty behind the pumps most afternoons - it was after all very quiet at that time of the day in Boston. One day I popped my head around the door to see the real reason why my services were not required. Several burly dockers, a couple of building site workers and my landlord husband were all sat in front of the television, staring intently at "Watch with Mother".

Staff of the Daily Herald Newspaper watching television in 1954.

✿ The Yorkshire writer, Ian McMillan, has a poem which starts, "Did you see, did you see; it was on TV, it was on TV." It's always been a favourite of mine, because in a very direct way it catches the sort of conversation which you would hear on a bus from Darfield to Barnsley in the early to mid 1950s. Then television was fresh and concentrated everyone's attention. A bus could be united by a subject which was known to all. The nearest parallel I can think of was the comment and opinion which was given by various voices on the top of a double-decker when the goal was clearly off-side and there were no action replays to prove it either way.

It has only recently occurred to me that the period when that was happening was transitory, for it was before you had a choice of programme. ITV didn't come along until 1955 and Sky existed only as science fiction. In those days everybody watched the same programme and those who didn't had only one alternative. Like Ian McMillan they sat, "Looking at the wall, looking at the wall."

✿ 'Opiate of the people' - that's what one of my aunties used to call television. She claimed it was a government ploy to stop people rioting or 'making babies'.

I don't know what she'd think today. I know what she meant when she said it. Harold Macmillan was Prime Minister then and my auntie had been brought up in a staunch Labour household. Political satire was in its infancy at the time but there was still a long way to go to "Spitting Image".

✿ There are some things that you cannot say on television because they seem tasteless and potentially offensive. One is to draw a parallel between the way in which the ship - "The Herald of Free Enterprise", sank and the philosophy encapsulated in the ship's name. I watched many hours of television news following that disaster and never once heard a commentator refer to the fact that it may have set off without the doors fully closed because it was rushing to ensure that the company didn't lose money. Putting profit before safety is exactly what is at the centre of free enterprise culture and yet no commentator said it. The irony, however, was not lost on most people I met and was currency in the pubs and at the dining tables I frequent.

The television producers would perhaps tell us that it was an example of self-censorship, but I cannot help thinking that the same scruples would not have come into play if this boat had been called "The Spirit of Islam", or "The Spirit of Socialism".

✿ I shall never ever forget the TV news pictures of the miners' strike on the day of the big demonstration at Orgreave. The clip where the policeman repeatedly hit an unarmed picket over the head with his truncheon is as clear in my mind's eye now as it was on the tea-time news that day. This is one picture of the strike I will remember till I die. Another is the press photo of the camera woman about to be struck by a mounted bobby looking like a medieval jouster. Combined, these two things serve to remind me whose side I am on.

✿ Reunification Day was supposed to be one of the greatest days in German history. As a family we sat down to watch at eight in the morning but by nine o'clock Kristina had got bored with all the politics and had gone back up to her room. We continued to watch right up to midnight, the precise moment when the two Germanys were reunited. For the final moments, Kristina came down to join us.

We are a town of ten thousand people, but no one had thought to call us into the town square to celebrate. Instead, we were content to sit in our armchairs and watch history being made from a camera angle. We now only go onto the streets out of habit; for carnival dressed in black cat masks, or for that American invention, halloween. We never go out to make history. A year before, the people of Halle and Leipzig went out in their thousands to object to their governments' actions. We watched it all on television. That, and the wall coming down, yet we would not go out into the open air and celebrate. Apart from one in Berlin and some in the border towns there were no community gatherings. Our only angle is the viewpoint of the camera. A little to the left and the police are beating the demonstrators. A little to the right and the forces of law and order are being attacked by anarchists.

&. There is no subject more likely to cause controversy than that of censorship. Whilst I think that most people are agreed that we must protect our children, it's a different matter when it comes to a choice for adults. My own view on this is less than straightforward. Whilst I concede that a free-for-all may well be detrimental to society, I find myself wondering about the machinations of it all. For instance, in order for someone to decide what I can and cannot watch, he or she will have to watch it first. I would then question that if they aren't tempted to go out and rape or murder someone, having viewed something of questionable taste, then why should I be? And what qualifies someone to be able to tell me what I am allowed to see in the privacy of my own home? I think that adults should be allowed to choose for themselves as long as people, most notably women and children, are protected from exploitation during the making of programmes.

&. According to my dad, only the television wrestling was true. Everything else was either fixed or a con. He even thought that the the racing results were fixed before the horses went into their starting stalls and that the football results were well-known before the kick-off.

On the night when man first landed on the Moon, I remember standing at the front door, staring up and pondering, 'Just think. At this very moment a man is walking on the Moon'. When I went back inside, the family were crowded around the box, watching the momentous event unfold. I told my dad what I'd just been thinking. He said. 'Don't be so bloody stupid lad. That's not real. It's a lie made up by the government in America to confuse the Russians'. He went on to describe how there was a huge television station in Hollywood which they had got up to look like the Moon. For a while I almost believed him, and it's funny, but just a couple of months ago I mentioned this to my brother and he said that he had believed it.

Passengers on the top deck of a London bus viewing a Pye portable television in 1960.

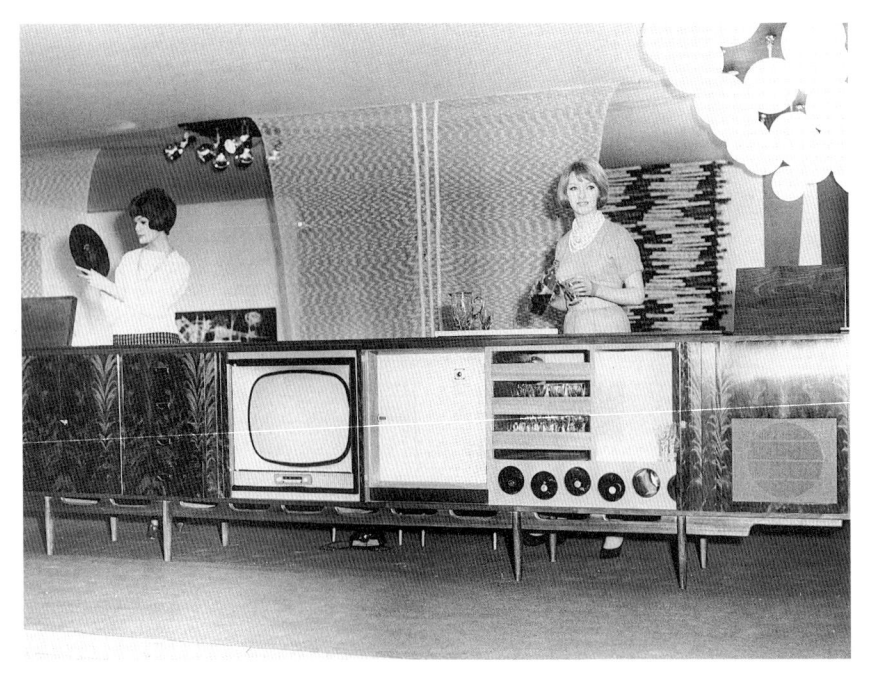

The Furniture Show, Earls Court, 1961. A cabinet incorporating a stereo Hi-Fi, TV set, cocktail cabinet, fridge and speakers. Cost? - £1,250

Since I work at the National Museum of Photography, Film and Television, people expect my set to be state-of-the-art. It isn't. It is a portable black and white set which usually sits on the floor in the corner of the living room. Why should I be into all the latest technology when I know quite clearly that I have been educated by totally different stimuli. Although I watched when the first man landed on the Moon, when I was ten and accept that this probably had some influence in making me take a science degree, years later, I was in no sense over-awed by the event as I had been in seeing the skeleton of a whale in the Royal Scottish Museum. That really was a wonderful sight. Why was I taken with it in a way that I have never been influenced by a television programme? That is a difficult one to answer but I think that it is because it is real, whereas the David Attenborough programmes are just shadows. I have watched the great classics - "Civilisation" and "The Ascent Of Man" - and recognise their quality, but they cannot compete for my imaginative attention with the bones of a great mammal who once was alive, but now is dead.

I was not allowed to stay up to watch the Moon landing live, but my Dad woke me up really early the next morning so that I could watch the telly before going to school. I can clearly recall the grey, blurry images of Neil Armstrong descending the steps of the Lunar Module. When I got to school I found that it was gripped by a sort of Moon fever. All of the kids, of course, had been watching the same pictures on television and the playground was full of little Armstrongs and Aldrins hopping around like kangaroos.

🍁 What worries me about the future with television is that the lines between fact and fiction are becoming extremely blurred. Sometimes I think it's a deliberate policy as well, because when it comes down to it, we're looking at the way things are presented to us, as much as what the content is.

I sat in a friend's apartment in san Francisco about five years ago. While outside in the street police sirens blared, I watched the all-star wrestling. Have you ever seen anything as ridiculous in your life? I flicked through the channels and settled on a film that showed a demonstration and police lights flashing. I guessed that the film was set somewhere in a futuristic Eastern Europe. After a few minutes, however, it dawned on me that I wasn't watching a feature film at all. This was a news item about the coming down of the Berlin Wall. All the camera angles suggested a movie. There was no voice-over or comment, just the shouts and cheers of people with hammers and crowbars in their hands, chipping away at the wall.

🍁 It always strikes me as a bit odd when people tell you that watching violence on television doesn't do anything to your kids. If you believe that then it seems bound to follow that you don't think that books have any influence for good or evil either.

Yet the world has been overturned by reading. Are they really saying that reading The Bible or The Koran hasn't influenced anyone or that Mein Kampf did not, in the tiniest way, influence the growth of National Socialism in Germany?

Yet what is reading? It's just a rather corny two-dimensional way of communicating, totally outclassed by television.

🍁 "Captain Pugwash"! If ever there was a series that sent up the idea of censorship, that was it. And we're talking children's programmes! How on earth the characters - Seaman Staines, Roger the Cabin Boy and Master Bates got passed the scissors is anybody's guess. Perhaps it was a more innocent time, perhaps nobody dare put two and two together. Or was it that the faceless person in charge had a sense of humour? We shall never know. But one thing is certain - the programme has never been repeated. Pity really - the stories were great, - Captain Pugwash himself looked like a direct descendant of Edward Teach - and the theme music was brilliant.

🍁 "Captain Pugwash" is a prime example of a 'false memory syndrome' linked to television. People often claim to remember things they've never seen because other people, TV shows and books etc. tell them about it. Johnny Ryan, the writer of Captain Pugwash, gets very cross about it. The First Mate had no name and the seamen were called Barnabas and Willy. This story has been doing the rounds for at lest ten years now.

Similarly, people remember TV's "Quatermass and the Pit" as set on the underground because the film was. TV's version wasn't. Another example is the 'glimpsed telegraph pole' in the "Robin Hood" credits - it doesn't exist though countless people claim to have seen it.

It's a similar phenomenon to the phrases, "Beam me up Scotty", "Elementary my dear Watson", "Silly Billy", and "Play it again Sam", being linked to "Star Trek", Sherlock Holmes, Denis Healey and "Casablanca", despite not being used, except by comedians and imitators. People aren't responding to the primary source, but to a response to the source - a manufactured, shared consensual myth.

🍁 "Send them a postcard Jim", Ada would bellow when we were subjected to a surfeit of jugglers, conjurors and ventriloquists. They were the staple ingredient of variety programmes and therefore were subjected to Ada's wrath. She would consult the 'Radio Times' and when they were on, the television would be discreetly covered with a cloth, large enough to indicate that the set was not in use, but not too large to hide the fact from visitors that a television set was part of her furniture.

We were rather surprised therefore when, on one of our visits to Jim and Ada's, her most hated programme was scheduled to appear and the television was left switched on. The title came on the screen and as the first jugglers were about to proceed to rotate the inevitable rings from hands and feet, Ada advanced on the set and with a grandiloquent flourish, turned it off. "There", she said, "If everybody did that, it would show them at the other end just what we thought of these silly programmes".

🍃 One of our neighbours is already complaining that scenes from soft porn movies are invading their viewing of "Coronation Street". It might or might not be true. The man with Sky who lives next door says that it's not him because they are not the sort of family who would watch such things, particularly in the early evening. To be quite honest, though, he is exactly the type who would - unclean shoes and a hole in his cardigan.

🍃 People go on about "Spitting Image" and say how it erodes institutions, clobbers politicians and brings the Royal Family into disrepute, but it's infantile compared with the first gloves-off satirical television programme, "That Was The Week That Was". I can remember being at parties in the early 1960s when everyone would rush home, forsaking hard liquor and a bit of spare, so that they could hear exactly what had happened to Macmillan's cabinet in the past week.

"That was the week that was , It's over let it go. Oh what a week that was", sang Millicent Martin, and from then on a talented team of comedians, singers and political commentators got stuck in and showed what a lot of establishment loonies - 'Super Mac', Lord Home (pronounced 'Hulme'), Home Secretary Brooke and Reginald Maulding - total fruitcakes - ran the country.

A lot go on about how satirical magazines full of investigative journalism and throaty disclosures brought down the Tory government, but it has to be remembered that votes matter and only a fraction of the population read "Private Eye". What they watched was late night Friday and late night Saturday television run by radicals such as David Frost and Bernard Levin.

🍃 Even though we didn't have television at home, my sister and I knew that "TW3", "That Was The Week That Was", was 'one of those programmes'. To compete with all our school friends we had to see it somewhere, somehow. At that time my auntie and uncle down the road had recently got a television. It was such a novelty for them that they wanted to share it with us if ever we visited. Of course my sister and I contrived to visit at the times "TW3" was showing. This worked well for a couple of weeks, then we were told by aunty, "Your uncle doesn't want you to watch 'that programme' again". When we asked why, we were eventually told it was too embarrassing for uncle to watch it with two adolescent schoolgirls. We giggled a bit, but didn't protest too much, it had been embarrassing for us too.

🍃 Oxford graduates term themselves MA (Oxon), so I don't see why I shouldn't describe myself as BA (OU, TV), because I learnt more off those low-budget "Open University" programmes than I have from a whole library of art books. The BBC's attitude to education is summed up by the way they treat those programmes. In no sense are they a priority; they get next to no publicity.

🍃 I try to avoid television at university, but I'm in the minority. As soon as "Neighbours" comes on the common room empties and everyone troops upstairs to the hall's television room. "Brookside", maybe. "Eastenders", yes. "The Bill", definitely. But "Neighbours"! There are a lot of English Literature students amongst them.

🍃 How fashions change. Look at the Open University programmes.

Twenty-five years ago, you tuned in in all seriousness to watch bearded men giving lectures in maths and sciences to tired-eyed students, who spent the rest of the day in factories and offices. Look at them now - they still show some of the same lectures, and they are hilarious. The same bearded men in flared trousers, kipper ties and flowered shirts. They talk about 'groovy molecules' and 'crazy logarithms' - at least if they don't they ought to do, and they stumble on platform shoes as they do their pieces to camera. How can people be expected to work all day and get up early to learn things off folk like that?

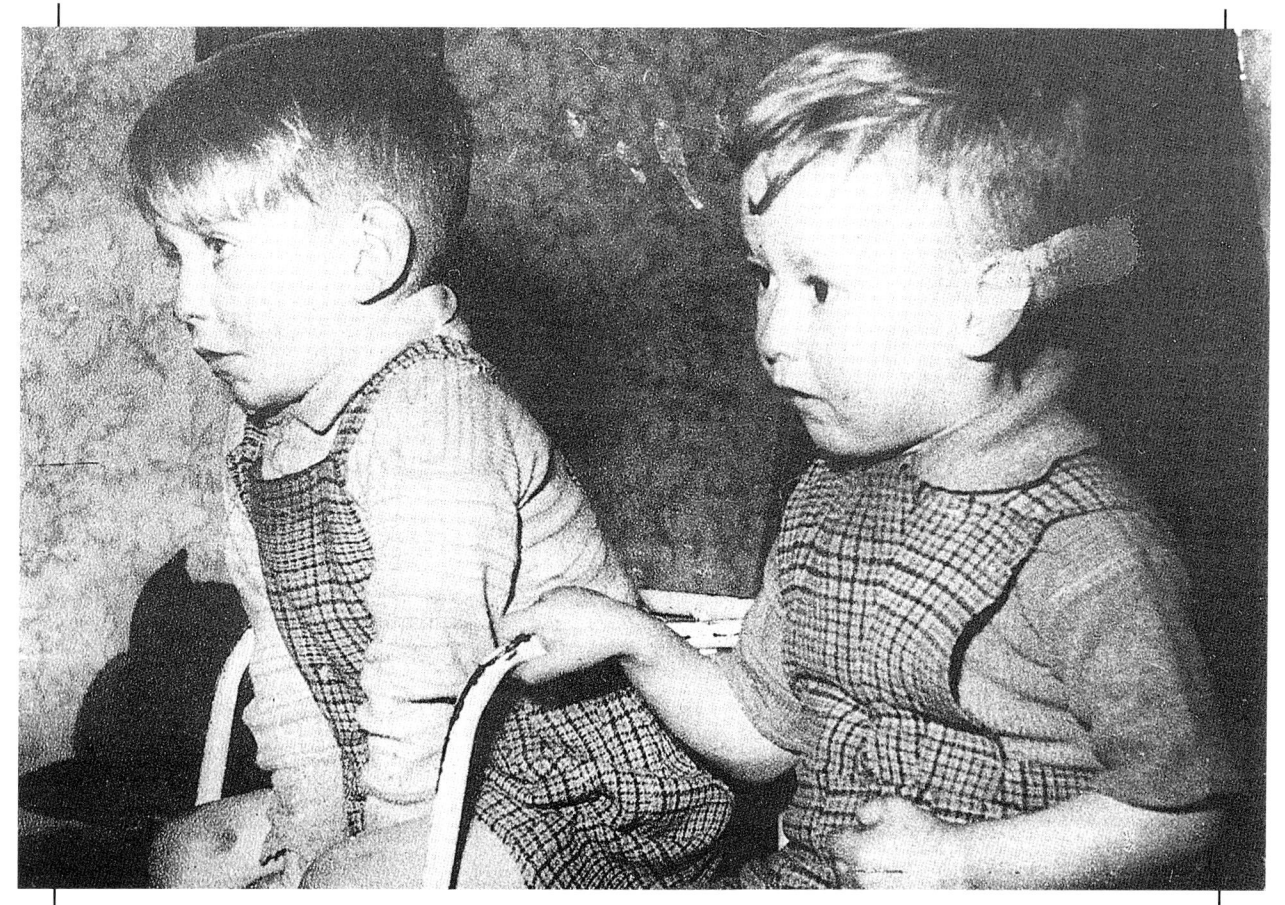

Children watching television, photograph by Jack Hulme.

🌿 Having young children has made me realise just how good some Open University programmes are. They get put on at such ridiculous times that I am sure hardly anyone discovers them by accident when flicking through the channels. The only reason I found them was because my two-year-old daughter insists on waking up at six in the morning. She likes to have the television on but isn't really bothered about what the programme is. So, instead of cartoons, we watch the Open University. On Saturday mornings there is a fascinating series of programmes about art and architecture in renaissance Florence and Siena. It is suprising what can be found in Florentine frescoes to keep a two-year-old happy.

❧ "Watch it, watch it. Now they are on Camera One and there's the switch to Camera Two." My husband and I often chat through the producer's job when we watch television. We have seen so much in our time that it comes naturally. I suppose what I most hate is the tendency for the crews to under-estimate our intelligence and, after that, their inability to let the camera be still. They are always moving in with no respect at all for the viewers' sensitivits. One minute you are on the soprano's face, the next you are panning in and travelling past her fillings, down and down her throat. How can they be so crass?.

What is true of the Promenade Concerts is also true of cooking programmes. They can't bear to look at the food being prepared; they assume that we have a burning desire to see the chef's face. Even when it's tap dancing or "Come Dancing", it's onto the smile and hold it. They seem to think that there is no need to show the neat little changeover if the woman has nice teeth.

❧ I only leave England with great reluctance, but a couple of years ago I was persuaded by my family that I should fly and visit Holland and Belgium. As I came down the staircase onto the runway, I cricked my back and by the time we reached the hotel the pain brought on by carrying heavy bags meant that I was useless. There was nothing to do but take a bath, forego the fleshpots of Amsterdam and watch television.

That night I lay back and saw my first episode of "All Creatures Great and Small", a nostalgic look at life in agricultural communities in the North of England and showing wonderful views of the countryside around Richmond. This was exactly the area I would have chosen to visit had may family not insisted that I widen my horizons. Travel, they say, broadens the mind.

❧ On New Year's Eve millions of continental people sit down with their families to watch a British movie, which is virtually unknown in Britain, yet whose viewing figures well exceed any film shown in England over the previous twelve months. If you get organised and live in the Baden-Wuttenberg region you can see it three times. German television carries it. Later, it goes out on the Swiss channel and it is also carried by one of the Austrian stations. Freddy Frinton's "Dinner for One" is hardly a cult movie. Too many people watch it for it to be that. It is, rather, an institution and now as Germanic as Stollen, real candles on the Christmas tree and venison for main course on Christmas day.

There's not much of a story. Frinton, a butler, is serving at table the lady of the house and several imaginary guests. To keep up the pretence that others sit with her, he drinks up all the glasses. As he gradually gets drunker, he trips over a bear skin rug, comes close to spilling the wine and eventually follows her up the stairs. When it is over people sit around saying how much they have enjoyed it and quoting the key line - "Same procedure as every year".

The family in front of the box, 1957.

Two schoolboys inspect the latest Philco combined radiogram and television at the Earls Court Radio Show, 1953.

CHAPTER THREE

STARS IN THEIR EYES

I come from a family whose television was switched on as long as somebody was in the front room. A family where talk was banned if "Emergency Ward 10" was on, where gossip petered out as soon as the "Coronation Street" theme tune struck up and where the art of conversation flew out of the window to the strain of catchphrases from Bruce Forsyth and Leslie Crowther. Even when the neighbours came round they would stand to attention at the back of the settee, hardly daring to breathe until the adverts started. Then they would talk in staccato bursts - but only if the advert wasn't somebody's favourite.

No wonder, then, that I've grown up to be a man who gushes with enthusiasm and talks like a rattle in half-hour bursts and then sits quietly as though somebody has twisted my ear and switched me off.

It comes from years of practice at playing 'dead lions'. A simple game with very few rules. Round about the time your mum and dad want to watch 'The Rag Trade' your dad tells you to prowl around the house, growling. Then, from his comfy armchair, pretending to be a big game hunter, he raises an imaginary rifle to his shoulder, narrows an eye and squeezes the trigger. BANG! You're dead. With one last agonised growl you collapse onto the fireside rug. This is where you remain for at least half an hour, motionless and silent. Then, of course, it's time for bed.

My family's attitude to TV has rubbed off on me. There is nothing I like more then 'Corra'. I love the game shows as well as those stupid quiz shows that wouldn't test the IQ of, er...well...er, the sort of people they get on those shows. I even watch daytime TV if I'm at home with the flu. I don't know why I do it, I think I'm probably built that way and I don't want to question this flaw too much. I'd sooner let the mystery be. Except, just now and then I'll say to myself, 'Well Ian lad, are you right in your head?' I did it not long ago. I was watching a very well put together BBC2 documentary about the Roman origins of the City of London. A cluster of all sorts of experts were being asked to theorise as archaeologists dug a trench, mud up to the top of their wellies. suddenly, i got an urge to switch to ITV. 'Whooska!', in the bat of an eye I went from Roman Londinium to Barrymore's couch, full of comical old ladies, precocious singing children and has-been music hall turns. I loved it!

One image I cherish more than any other when I think about television is a Monday evening image. Damp washing hangs on a wooden rack just below ceiling level in our front room. A Westminster chimer tick-tocks on a mantlepiece and below that burns a big coal fire right up the chimney back. In the big chair next to the boxed-in gas meter sit my Grandad, puffing on his Peterson. On the three-seater sits my brothers, my Auntie Alice and my Gran. On the flickering black and white in the corner, Hughie Green means what he says, most sincerely and introduces a parade of old comics and precocious brats. Meanwhile, connected to the same power supply as the TV by a dangerous looking 3-way adaptor, my mother's iron swishes to and fro. As it glides over assorted pillow cases and pinnies, my mother's beautiful singing voice soars up to the corrugated pelmet. 'Love is a many splendoured thing'. Sadly, a TV talent opportunity never knocked on our front door, or. if it did, we didn't hear it for the television.

I suppose I've been a bit more fortunate. In recent years I've made quite a lot of appearances on the box, both as a writer and presenter of programmes, mostly on the BBC. I ought to say at this point that I speak with a strong West Yorkshire accent. In fact, a lot of people accuse me of 'putting it on' and making myself even broader and that's how I get on. Not my Gran. She thinks I can't help it and, after one appearance on BBC2's Late Show, she sat me down next to her on the settee and offered the following advice. 'Look, love. It might pay you to spend a bit of your wages on elocution lessons. You can't keep theeing and thying on television. Folk won't understand thee.' Never mind. There might yet be a place on the couch alongside Barrymore for me. 'Ladies and gentlemen, introducing comical old dialect speaker....'.

Ian Clayton

🕭 I had been on television before but never with a known name. Richard Whiteley was more pleasant than I had expected - he told me he had been to Cambridge and had been a reporter for twenty five years - and then wandered off. Eventually he came to rest in the centre of the castle bailey gate surrounded by assistant producers, sound technicians and two camera men. I retired and stood with a group of onlookers around the custodian's shelter.

It was an assorted group and this was appropriate. Most were silent, adopting the "What a lot of silly buggers" mode, but one woman definitely wasn't. She kept saying things like, "He's lovely is our Richard" and, "Don't Richard look smashing standing there". She called him "our Richard" and at first I thought that he was family, but as she went on I realised that she was just a fan. After a time, I was called, did my piece, shook hands and moved back into the crowd as Richard Whiteley strode off to the editor's van.

"He didn't look at us. He didn't even wave", the woman said. She was close to tears.
"Why should he?" I wondered.

🕭 My parents thought that I had gone to Chloe's for the night to catch up on revision and I wasn't going to disillusion them. I got home on Sunday night. Dad greeted me.
'Have you had a good time?
'Yes, really nice.'
'Did you go up town last night?'
'No. We revised French.'
'You didn't go out dancing?'
'No. We revised.'
'That's funny because there were a lot of close up shots on a programme I watched last night about rave clubs. There were a couple of young girls who could have been your doubles. What's more, one was wearing exactly that dress you were so pleased about when you bought it last week.'

Me and Richard Whiteley.

🍂 I made a short appearance while "Champion House" was being filmed in the mill where I worked. How long ago I can't remember. I was the operative worker who took Wilfred Pickles to the First Aid when he was supposed to have hurt his arm or hand. If you blinked your eye you missed me. Not much to brag about, but it was fun preparing and meeting Wilfred and Mabel.

🍂 During the time "Follyfoot" was on I got married and, naturally, posted some wedding cake to Gillian Blake and Steve Hodson. I loved watching those weekly episodes starring Gillian Blake as Dora and Steve Hodson playing the role of Steve. I got a reply from Steve, who told me all about himself and Gillian. Steve played parts in many other TV stories, and later went on to work on BBC Radio. Gillian, I think, retired from TV to have a baby. She had her own horse, which also took part in "Follyfoot". I loved being involved with them, though only in a small way. The last time I saw them was as guests on "This Is Your Life". I would love to see these fine actors again on TV, but most of all would like to meet them or perhaps get to know where they are now.

Dicky Howett, aged 11, beside an ATV Pye MK3 camera, Southend-On-Sea, 1956.

🍂 Not for me a football star, train driver or airline pilot. I wanted to be a television cameraman when I grew up! Well, as it turned out, I never made it as a TV cameraman, nor, indeed, as my wife will attest, have I really grown up! To compensate, nowadays, I collect antique studio television cameras.

My obsession began when watching 'The Appleyards', a 1953 BBC soap, broadcast at teatimes. One of the episodes had a dreaded 'technical hitch'. On this occasion the picture suddenly panned across the studio revealing, for a delicious second or two, lots of mysterious equipment, including a massive television camera. That's for me, I thought! I would just love to have a go on one of those. But back then I was only a weedy kid, so how could I achieve my ambition?

To get near to some cameras, I applied for studio audience tickets to live shows such as 'The Billy Cotton Band Show' and 'The Ted Ray Show'. Of those programmes the memory has faded. Not suprising since I spent the whole time ogling the cameras. However, one thing did strike me about the old BBC Television Theatre. That was how small and cluttered the place was. On screen the stage looked enormous. In reality, with all the cameras and cranes and lights, the available floor space was little more than that of a double-width garage.

Then, in 1956, the moment came. I actually touched a real live television camera. This was courtesy of ATV who made a Saturday habit (in the absence of sporting attractions - the BBC had those) of transmitting carnivals and beauty contests from exotic places such as Southend-On-Sea. The outside broadcast van was parked on the promenade and the equipment was 'resting' alongside, awaiting the next transmission. I sauntered up to a camera and reverentially touched a lens. At that point an ATV technician popped up and told me tactfully to 'bugger off!'.

Nowadays, forty years later, I have my own ex-ATV camera, along with about ten others, all of which I shrewdly rent out for use as vintage props in commercials, films and TV. The best part is, if the shot calls for it, I get to play the cameraman!

Dicky Howett with his EMI 2001 camera in his living room.

In the beginning there were fanzines, typed on some ancient remmington and run off on a ditto machine somewhere. They weren't much, but they were the best way for fans of cult shows like Star Trek to communicate with one another.

These led, in turn, to conventions where spotty teenagers in homemade costumes could speak Klingonese to one another. If they were particularly lucky a 'real star' from the show might turn up to sign autographs and answer questions. From these humble beginnings in the 1960s, fanzines and conventions grew in scope and sophistication throughout the 1980s.

Inevitably, commercial concerns got involved. While their conventions were the slickest and attracted the biggest name stars, they were also huge, impersonal affairs where you could queue for hours for a ten second photo opportunity with a haggard star. Fan culture grew and diversified but the conventions took on a more impersonal air.

Then the Internet was born. True, you couldn't actually communicate with the 'stars' but the 'net did allow instant access to thousands of people all over the world who shared similar interests. In those glorious early years of the global community, most of the people who had access worked in business, the government or universities. Today, those sectors still dominate, though commercial providers are beginning to make inroads into the home computing market.

Newsgroups were the first and most accessible resource for fans. Newsgroups are arranged in a hierarchy with the 'alt' groups being the easiest to set up. You can find 'alt.blackadder', 'alt.prisoner' and 'alt.brady-bunch', to name just a few out of literally dozens. The next grouping that appeals to television fans is the 'rec' (short for recreation) group. These groups are usually much more general, such as 'rec.arts.tv.soaps' and 'rec.arts.tv.uk.' Traffic on this last group became so busy that it recently split into 'rec.arts.tv.uk.sci-fi.' and 'rec.arts.tv.uk.comedy.', 'rec.arts.tv.uk.coronation-street.' etc. There are those, however, who complain that public access newsgroups are not personal enough or are too general to appeal to fans of a specific show. For these people, mailing lists are the best way to communicate. Mailing lists differ from newsgroups in that they use simple e-mail to send an individual's posting to everyone who has subscribed to the group. You must subscribe to the group in order to receive e-mail. While most mailing lists are open to everyone, some are closed and new members must be nominated by someone already in the group. Until recently, one of the biggest problems with mailing lists was actually finding the subscription address in the first place. These were sometimes posted under FAQs (frequently asked questions) but tracking down elusive addresses could be a tedious and time-consuming process.

The latest innovation on the 'net - the world wide web - has made the process of locating information for fans much simpler. Web pages for many popular and even a few obscure television programmes are popping up all over the 'net. These pages include fan-provided episode guides, actor information and even photographs and sound clips. Most importantly, the web provides easy links to other sites containing similar information. At the moment, anyone with an internet connection and a bit of time on their hands can create their own web page and get it linked to other pages and search engines. While the dramatic increase in 'net traffic threatens to end this virtual democracy, internet die-hards are fighting for freedom from regulation. Only time will tell. At the moment, however, the 'net provides fans with an eager and knowledgeable audience throughout the world. Every possible taste is catered for and it is the obscure question indeed that fails to get a response.

The Television Toppers admire a Pye 27inch television, the largest set at the 1953 Earls Court Radio Show.

When television reached the House of Commons, we were told that it would end up with MPs making over-long speeches, so that they could draw attention to themselves. This doesn't seem to have happened; that's probably because many Members of Parliament have always had a tendency towards over blown rhetoric and the presence of a camera has made little difference.

If Parliament has been influenced by television, it is in the seating arrangements. One of our local MPs often appears on the set because he positions himself one row behind the opposition front bench and ensures that he is in shot when Margaret Beckett or Tony Blair rises to speak. In this way when he goes into the Club on Saturday night, there is always someone present who says, "I saw you in Parliament this week".

Television helps camouflage the fact that on two occasions that week he had travelled North at 69.8 pence per mile - at £265.24 a time; a profitable journey - so that he could sleep in his own bed.

🍀 In the very first episode of "Coronation Street", when Pat Phoenix looked into the mirror and said, "Eee..., Elsie Tanner tha' looks ready for't knackers yard", we all fell about laughing, not least my late mother, whose name was Elsie Tanner. She certainly took some stick after that!

🍀 I came over to Bradford from Malta in September 1960, when I was seventeen years old. I arrived at my brother's house in Bradford at about eleven o'clock in the morning and, although he and his wife were expecting me, they did not know the exact time of my arrival. Consequently, when I got to their house they were out. A neighbour of theirs told me that they had gone to visit my sister-in-law's mother and tried to give directions as to how to find them. As I am a complete stranger to Bradford, and indeed England, I decided to wait on the doorstep until they got home. I sat there for eight hours. It was early evening before they eventually arrived home. My sister-in-law hardly had time to greet me before she opened the door, rushed inside and put the TV on. We had to sit and watch "Coronation Street" before a proper welcome was given to me. This episode, along with the smell of coal fires and fish and chip shops, will always be my first memory of TV, Bradford and the UK.

🍀 I believe it was around 1982 when the Co-op in Birstall market place was officially opened by Pat Phoenix - Elsie Tanner of "Coronation Street". I was there at the opening and unfortunately I had broken my wrist and had it in a plaster cast. I went to Pat to get her autograph and she signed her name on my plaster cast. I have still got the cast which was taken off my wrist. I have kept the pot to this day as a souvenir.

🍀 There's usually a couple of guides on duty and so we sometimes ask people to gather round so that we can explain things in a more structured way. One of our number then says that he will give "enough facts to bore your mother-in-law", and embarks on a description of the origin of the series and of "the street". By the end, people not only know that this is the third street to be built, but also that there are 10,000 cobbles - which always seems a lot to me - and that although the houses are of brick and the roofs of slate, the chimney pots are of polystyrene. This is because there are no partition walls between the houses.

He also points out that there is a cross on the street by the telephone box and if you stand on it, then you get the best photograph of yourself in the Rovers Return Inn doorway, don't and you'll see yourself with the letters "urn Inn" above your head. To emphasise the point, he somehow manages to pronounce this "urine".

🍀 At about four-thirty, people begin to go into the alley at the back of the street and hang about waiting to see the actors come out from the rehearsal studios. They are usually lucky and occasionally individuals will come over and talk. It's not a lot different from hanging about to see Lady Di really. It is in everybody's interest to keep the PR going, but it also happens because the majority of the actors are genuinely nice people.

That's how the street works and why the show has been successful for so long. It is based on the development of character and not so much on story line. It is centred and therefore rings true. If it doesn't there is something wrong.

We take the views of our visitors seriously. One once pointed out that when a man goes out from the bar of the Rovers for a jimmy-riddle, he must do it in the lounge of number three, because the wall of the pub was the wall of the next house. Our designers took this on board and when they next did modifications to the street, they built an entry between the two buildings.

🍀 They all do the same, lift the letter box, cup their hands and look through the windows, try the door knob and ring the bell. Some will stand in the doorway of the Rovers Return to have their pictures taken, others will go into the working phone box on the corner and phone relatives to say "Guess where I am phoning from - Coronation Street". If they buy a first class stamp in the gift shop, they can post it in the letterbox by the corner

❧ I can answer questions from the days of Ena Sharples, Martha Longhurst and Minnie Caldwell. I will travel anywhere to meet a member of the cast. The first one I met was Johnny Briggs, who plays Mike Baldwin; he was opening a jewellers in Castleford. I then met Chris Cooke, that's Mark Redmon, and recently met Sarah Lancashire, who stars as Raquel, and after a couple of minutes we were talking as if we had known each other for years. I told Sarah how big a fan I was and she told me that Liz Dawn and Bill Tarmey were opening a shop in Leeds the following Saturday. I met them in Leeds Market. I was talking to Bill when someone said, "Where's Liz?". She had disappeared. She was found on the outside market buying strawberries. Bill said to me, "Do you know, she think's she's at Wimbledon!"

My ambition is to meet all the "Coronation Street" characters.

On the steps of the Rover's Return.

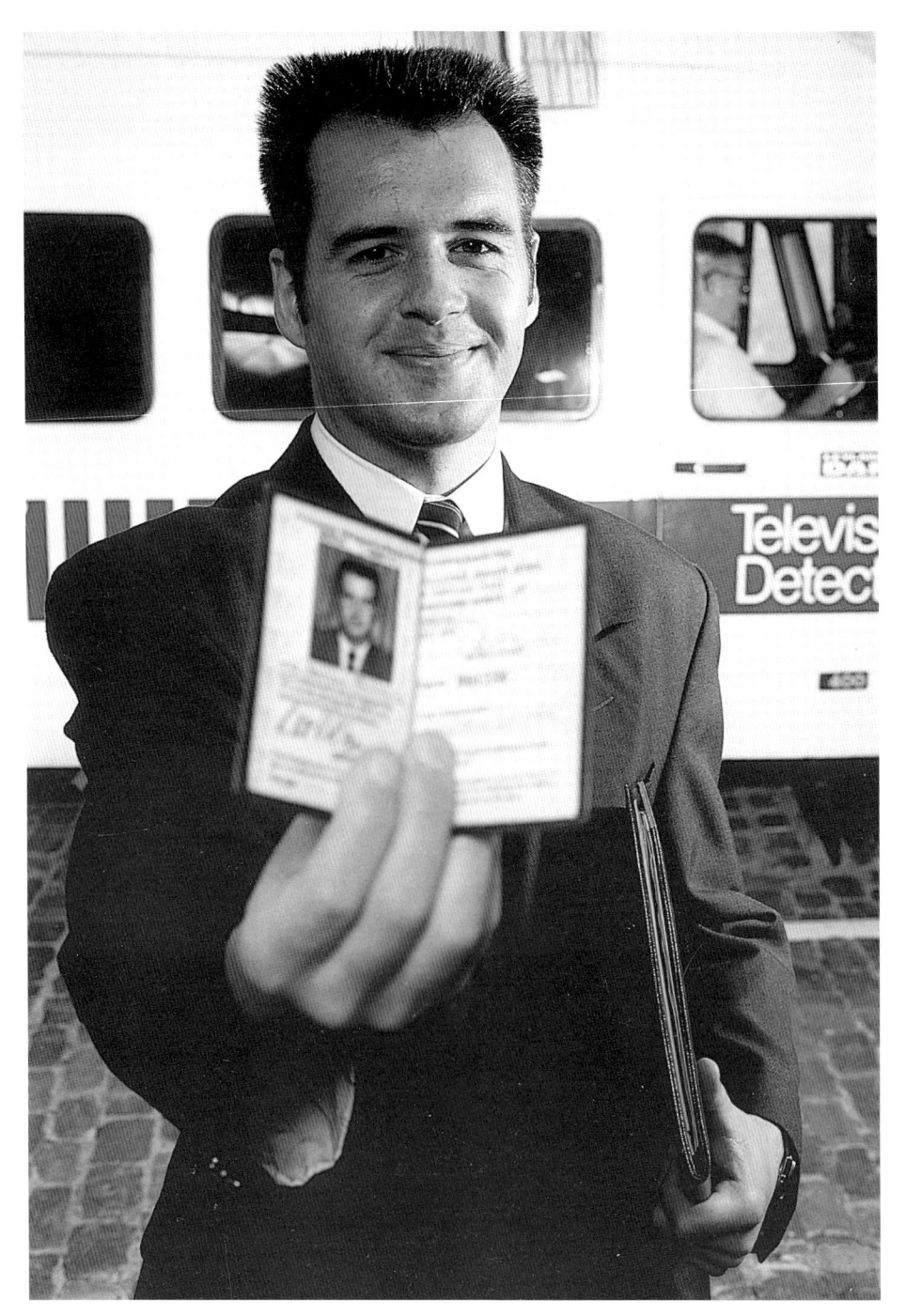

A TV licence enquiry officer.

🙢 This guy who had been a roadie for Thin Lizzy offered me a room in his council house on the Airedale Estate. Some people thought it was a bit rough but I was desperate for a roof over my head. He said his house had two big bedrooms and I was welcome to move in with him. The only sticks of furniture he had were a gas boiler he used as a table with a piece of plywood over, two old chairs, a bookcase and an old battered dansette record player. I didn't even have a mattress and there was only one lightbulb.

After a couple of months we got a TV, but we couldn't afford the licence and we were always dreading the time when the detector van came round - it always seemed to be on these estates and not on the posh housing estates. Sure enough, one day it came. The inspector came up to the door and knocked. John looked through the curtain and told me to run down and hide it in the garden. I hid it behind a tree. We told the inspector we didn't have a set and there was a long argument on the doorstep because his records showed we did have one. We let him look around the house and he was eventually satisfied that we didn't have a telly. As it turned out, he was right. I went down to the bottom of the garden and it had been pinched.

🙢 My television licence was always due just before Christmas, so one year I decided to risk leaving it until January. Of course I completely forgot about renewing it until about the middle of February, when I answered a knock at the door and saw the detector van. The man at the door asked if I had a television licence. I said I did, knowing damn well I hadn't. I reckoned to search for it and then went back to the door and told them I couldn't find it. The bloke at the door said he could confirm that we didn't have a licence. I tried to get out of it by saying there must have been a mix-up because I'd definitely given my wife the money to get a licence. The bloke at the door was really nice and he told me to go down to the post office the next day and get a licence and to have it back-dated to December when the last one ran out. The I had to send it off with a letter and explain about the misunderstanding. So I did this and a few weeks later got my licence back with a letter saying thank you for sending it and as it was back-dated to December, they would take no further action. I was bloody relieved about that.

The following year I thought I was being crafty by leaving it again until January, but making sure I didn't leave it any later. I reckoned the detector van wouldn't be round until February. Anyway, about the middle of January, I went down to the post office. The woman behind the counter asked when the old licence had run out, so I said December, but I wanted the new licence to start from January, because we hadn't had a television since the last one ran out. A couple of weeks later, I got a letter from them saying thank you for the payment for the TV licence, but that they had back-dated it to December.

TELEVISION LICENCES

The selling of licences in order to fund the BBC began in 1922 when the Postmaster General issued the first licences on the instruction of the Home Office. At that time, of course, there were only radio licences. It was not until 1946 that the first combined radio and television licences were issued. These first TV licences cost £2.

Licence detector vans also date back to the days of wireless. Today, as well as a fleet of vans equipped with the latest detection equipment, every enquiry officer also has a hand-held detector for use in areas where the vans cannot go, such as blocks of flats.

There are currently nearly twenty-one million TV licences in force in Britain. It is estimated, however, that this still leaves about two million people who have a set but no licence. In 1994, four hundred thousand licence evaders were caught - over one thousand every day. Licence fees account for 90% of the BBC's income, currently £1.7 billion each year.

1952.

1969.

Morris Oxford detector van, 1962-1968.

Leyland Daf detector van, 1991 - present.

🔹 The rumours spread like wildfire. I remember being about eight years old at the time and going out with the other children in the street on the look-out for the TV detector van. Upon seeing it, everyone would scatter to their respective homes, where frantic comings and goings followed. In our house, the TV found a new home in the pantry. The sideboard, where it used to reside, became a display of all the ornaments gathered from every nook and cranny. The all clear was eventually given and total calm returned. The TV was then restored to its rightful place and normal services resumed as quickly as possible.

🔹 I once called on a house and bumped into a housewife who was just leaving to go shopping. When I asked to see her television licence, she said that she was in a rush and asked me to come back a bit later when her husband would be at home. She said that she had put the licence behind the clock on the mantlepiece.
When I called back, the husband was at home. When I asked for the licence he said that he didn't know where his wife had left it. I told him to try looking behind the clock. He was totally gobsmacked - 'I knew your detector vans were good, but I had no idea they were that good!'

🔹 I was once asked to wait on the doorstep for a couple of minutes while the dog was put out the back. "He gets a bit frisky with strangers", I was told. Once inside the lounge I noticed that the curtains had been closed, even though it was the middle of the afternoon. When I glanced through a crack in the curtains I saw an elderly woman struggling down the garden path, bent double under the weight of a television set. When I pointed this out to the householder she replied 'Don't mind her. It's just Granny!'

🔹 When I went into the living room I saw a coffee table in the corner. This was covered in dust, apart from a perfectly-shaped square patch - just the same size as a television set. Under the coffee table there was a video recorder, flashing away. When I asked the householder about it he replied 'Oh Yes. I only keep that for the clock.'

🔹 I was checking out whether the holder of a black and white licence really did have a monochrome set. When I saw the television it was obvious that it was a colour receiver, although, at the time, it was showing a black and white picture. Adjusting the controls, I managed to get a good colour picture, much to the feigned amazement of the owner of the set - 'After all these years. I never knew it was a colour set!'

🔹 One young chap said that although he had a set he hadn't used it for months. When I pointed out to him that the set was still warm he replied 'Of course it is. That's where the cat sits.'

🔹 I am sitting, waiting for a knock on the door. I know they will come because I was told as much. I was out doing my shopping at Aldi, when a man pulled up alongside me in his car. He said, "I'm just waiting for your address to come up on my computer again and I'll be paying you a little visit". He can come if he likes. I'm prepared to go through it all over again. Let me put you in the picture. In 1988 I got my first satellite television system. I suppose it was the fascination with other countries and languages that set me off. I can be transported from my front room in Albert Street to anywhere in Europe and, when I get a bigger dish, to places in Asia. My problems started one Monday evening in January 1993.
"Good evening, I'm a Television Licence Inspector."
"I've been expecting you", I said and went on politely, "Take a seat, Sharon is just watching "Neighbours".
The bloke sat down and asked, "Do you have a licence for your television set?"
I told him "No". He then asked, "Is it a colour set ?", (which was a bit of a daft question because it was right under his nose).
Anyway, I said "Yes". He asked me then, "When was the set installed?" I told him that it was installed on 17 April 1992. He went on to tell me that I could be prosecuted under the Wireless and Telegraphy Act 1949. I told him that I only received satellite broadcasts and at that he up and left.

I would willingly buy a television licence if I had a television, but while I openly admit to watching television programmes, I maintain that I watch them on a monitor attached to some satellite receiving equipment. I cannot receive any terrestrial broadcasting, that includes BBC and ITV. Before you start wondering, Sharon was watching a repeat of "Neighbours" on Sky.

I received a summons to Pontefract Magistrates. I wasn't worried, I fully intended to defend. My defence rested on the plain fact that I wasn't technically using a TV. I had instructed the engineer to remove the tuner when he delivered it and, what's more, I had a letter from the engineer which stated quite clearly that I was unable to receive domestic stations. The case was adjourned. I paid two further visits to Pontefract Magistrates and I was finally ordered to pay for a licence within seven days, or appeal to the Crown against conviction. In the meantime, I was fined £133. I didn't pay.

On 1 November 1993, I made my appearance in front of Judge Norman Jones QC at Leeds. At the back of my mind, I prepared for prison, but I truly believed that given a fair hearing, I would win. I sat through two hours of extremely complicated legal proceedings. Armed only with a copy of the "Penguin Guide to the Law", my letter from the TV engineer and my utter belief that I was in the right, I stood up in court to defy the system.

There was a lot of to-ing and fro-ing and then, shortly before 7.30, the judge ruled in my favour, saying, "We think in this case the prosecution has been unable to establish that the apparatus in that house and on that day, fell within sub-section one of the 1949 Act". With those words, he allowed my appeal.

My immediate reaction was that I had struck a blow for the little man in the street. Now I just feel wronged. I'm unemployed and had to penny pinch to get to and from court, then there was the letter writing, postage, envelopes, photocopying; even though I didn't pay a fine, I've probably paid as much in costs.

There is one thrill though. When I tried to get solicitors to help me right at the beginning, nobody wanted to touch me with a barge pole. I proved I could do it. As my dad has always drilled into me, "Stand up for yourself".

I came home and wrote in black felt tip on my memo board, "I won", and it's still there. I also took out the brown manilla folder containing all my legal papers and wrote across it, "I beat the system". That's when the news and media interest started. My phone number is ex-directory, but somehow the newspapers got hold of it. Features appeared in "The Sun", "Star", "Mirror", "Guardian", "Telegraph", "Mail", "Independent", "Today", and of course "The Pontefract and Castleford Express", who had followed my case since the beginning and had been very supportive. "Calendar" TV came and did a piece; unfortunately, I didn't see it because I can't get Yorkshire Television on my monitor.

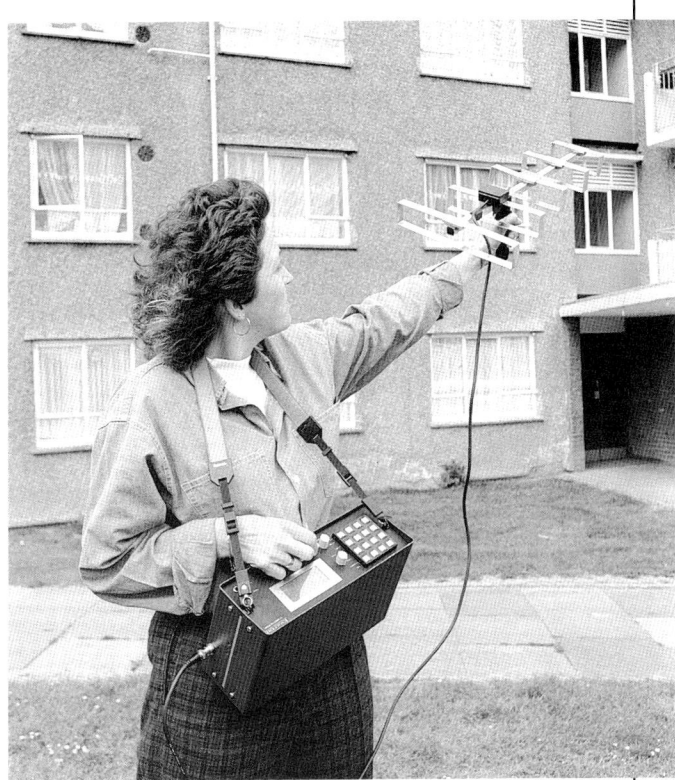

Using a hand held detector.

❧ A number of years ago my husband was walking down King Edward Street when he recognised a familiar face. He said, "How do", and received the answer, "How do mate". He chatted for a while, but could not place the man and wondered where he had met him before. When he arrived home, he realised it was Bill Maynard he'd been talking to. Whenever Bill appeared on TV after that, Bob always said, "It's my mate".

When I see him on Sundays in "Heartbeat", I think, "That's Bob's mate".

❧ You don't see television stars where I come from. So, when I saw Chris Evans walking in front of me I had to do something. In the end, I walked up to him, said 'I think that you are very good' and rushed away to hide my shame.

❧ Jeremy Beadle has got a lot to answer for. Of course, some of the clips on "You've Been Framed" are extremely funny, but we're not laughing along with people, we're laughing at them. Little did Andy Warhol know when he said that everyone will be famous for fifteen minutes, that within thirty years, the length of fame would be down to fifteen seconds. And the lengths some people will go to for their fifteen seconds fame is extraordinary. It's quite obvious that many of the so-called videoed mishaps you see on that programme are set up. With increased access to new technology, the cheapness of top quality video cameras and editing equipment, and the ease with which it can be used, we have a real opportunity to make quality television with ordinary people. Instead, what do we get? ... dog rough clips of the family pet stealing Auntie Aggie's slippers and Uncle Norman falling drunkenly onto the cake at Cousin Peter's wedding reception, week after week after week. I think it's more a case of, "We've Been Framed".

❧ On April 12, 1959, the first pre-recorded church service was shown. It was the centenary service for Saltaire United Reform Church. My husband was then the organist and choirmaster. I was in the congregation. Since all TV was black and white then you lost all of the colourful splendour of the church interior - blues and warm woodwork. My cream coat showed up well but my cerise velvet hat and my brown hair were inextricably mingled. We had to re-record the first ten minutes due to a technical fault. We were allowed to go into the TV van and see them working. We had the service professionally recorded on 78rpm records for the congregation to buy. They used my voice for the introduction.

Britain's first mains/battery portable TV, made by E.K. Cole Ltd in 1955.

The latest model.
Toni O' Dowd carries a Ferranti 17 inch portable TV, 1959.

My Father passed away in 1952, leaving £100 in his will. My Mum and I debated long and hard what to do with the money and eventually decided to buy a television. It cost us £74 - most of the money we had.

One evening we were watching "Double Your Money". After the show had finished an advert came on, asking for new contestants for the show. Being a football-mad fourteen year old, I decided to apply, answering questions on association football. I sent off my postcard and a couple of weeks later a letter arrived, inviting me to go to a selection interview at the Adelphi Hotel in Liverpool. There I met Hughie Green who asked me questions about football. A few weeks later I received another letter, this time informing me that I had been chosen as a contestant for "Double Your Money" and inviting me to the Rediffusion studios in London.

My Uncle and my Mum went with me. In the end, we had to go back five or six times and I won £500. I decided not to go for the £1,000 question - name the players in the Newcastle United team in the 1951 Cup Final. What was the half-time and full-time score and who were the scorers? - I would have got the answer but had decided not to risk it.

Bernard Owen, aged 14, appears on "Double Your Money", 1956.

For a while I was treated as a celebrity. I remember saying to one reporter that I would like to buy ice creams for all my mates at school. Lyons, the ice cream people, must have heard about this because a few days later a van delivered a case of ice cream to my house for me to take to school and share out. I also remeber getting a lot of letters from people all over the country. All very nice, kind souls who said how much they had enjoyed watching me on the programme. I was treated to seeing Liverpool play Fulham at Anfield, courtesy of the Liverpool Daily Post and Echo. After the game I was taken into the dressing room and introduced to the Liverpool players, including Billy Liddell, my favourite player.

As for the money. It came in very handy, of course, and we were able to buy lots of things that we could not otherwise have afforded. I wanted an electric train set - a Hornby OO. My mum said that I would soon get fed up with it. She was right. My interest lasted about a week. Later that year, I appeared in a Christmas Special edition of "Double Your Money". I was the question master and Hughie Green dressed up as a little boy contestant. I tried a few times to get on to other quiz shows but as soon as I told them that I had won on "Double Your Money" I was turned down.

Schoolboy Bernard Owen waves his cheque for £500.

Test card F (Courtesy of the BBC)

Twenty eight years ago I had some photographs taken. I remember nothing of the session, except eating sandwiches. I cannot recall if I realised that I might appear on television.

When I changed schools others did not believe it was me on the 'Testcard', so I used to take in the clown to show them, to prove that it was actually me, or tell them that I was going to be in the newspapers or on television.

Newspapers and T.V. occasionally contact me as everybody has heard of the 'Testcard Girl'. I am now married with 2 young children and it has nothing to do with my life now.

❧ I grew up in a non-musical family. I was a curious child and, before starting school, would entertain myself by watching the BBC schools broadcasts. I recall one morning when the programmes finished and gave way to this odd-looking pattern of circles and squares accompanied by, to me, superb music which had me totally entranced. With the excited air of one confronted with the most stimulating thing that life can offer, I called to my mother, demanding to know what this 'thing' was. "Oh, it's the test card", she replied with the uninterested air of one determined to ground me in my excitement. It was, and still is, the music which held my attention. It would not have mattered what the visual accompaniment was. The wonders of line-output transformers, high-frequency streaking and aerial installation were quite lost on me. I was listening to the world's finest session musicians playing a cross-section of music that I had hitherto not been exposed to. Jazz, Latin American, light orchestral and classic were there, largely uninterrupted, for anyone who cared to enjoy. Without any doubt, it was listening to this music that made me want to become a professional musician. I have been since leaving school and I have been privileged to work with many of the finest artists and musicians in the world.

Helping to found the Test Card Circle back in 1989 was a great achievement. It provided the opportunity for an aspect of television which, until more recent times had been given more hours of broadcasting time than any programme, to become not only respectable but to be documented properly for the first time. It should be seen as a worthy part of the whole gamut of British television history.

One of the fascinating aspects of the music used by the BBC for trade test purposes was the contractual agreements surrounding it. It was not possible to obtain any of it commercially although it was played, day in and day out on TV and also on radio. This was because the BBC were limited in the number of commercial records they could play by the 'needle time' agreement with the Musicians' Union. Suffice it to say that without this seemingly cumbersome restriction, it would not have been possible to have heard some of the finest music ever recorded and, who knows, I might have ended up as a solicitor!

THE TEST CARD

Most people are familiar with the television test card but few, I suspect, would be able to explain its purpose. Test cards were originally introduced following demands by television dealers and repairers. Since, at first, programmes were only broadcast for a few hours each day, they needed a picture of some sort at other times in order to demonstrate their sets or identify faults. The lines and patterns on a test card are carefully designed to give an accurate indication of the performance of the set and to check such things as aspect ratio, contrast, scanning linearity and synchronisation separation.

Today, the coming of almost twenty-four hour broadcasting means that the test card is not seen so often. Repairers now carry around electronic signal generators which means that they no longer have to rely on a broadcast test signal.

Over the years, there have been a number of different test cards. The one that most people recognise, the young girl playing noughts and crosses, is known as Test Card F. It was introduced in 1967.

Test cards are a source of fascination and nostalgia to some people, as is the light music that was played during test transmissions. In Britain there are two societies that cater for these interests - the Test Card Circle and the Test Card Club.

❧ You can see the beginnings of interactive television in those programmes where you are given a telephone number for a "yes" vote and one for a "no" vote. There they are using two pieces of equipment in one house; a domestic telephone and a family television set. Soon every house will have these two services in one machine. That's when you will be able to choose an alternative ending to plays and other fantasys. Let Rhett decide to go with Scarlett back to the homestead and let Michael Jackson be with Ms Presley for ever and ever. Then a black Desdemona can strangle a white Moor.

❧ Fancy having your whole life recorded? Aren't you just sick of seeing these blokes with camcorders held with one hand up to their good eye; you don't see many women doing it, do you?. Children are being filmed at birth, before they're washed, cleaned up and placed delicately into lacy baby clothes. Little Tommy's first tumbling steps are captured for ever. Auntie Alice drops her teeth as she sleeps in her rocking chair, having a fireside nap before "Neighbours" comes on, and she gets filmed. Cousins get videoed in their school uniforms. Mum becomes a star with a Fairy Liquid bottle in her hand and Gran pops up in a deckchair on her holidays at Blackpool. And how long will it be before the camcorder men start filming Grandad's funeral.

What is it all for? Just so some daft prat can show their silly blooming films to us, or send a clip to Granada Television. It was bad enough when we had to visit relatives to see their holiday snaps and be bored all evening. Now we have to sit round their tellies and coo and gurgle when we see our Maureen's new baby, laugh at Auntie's mishaps and rock too and fro reckoning to be madly amused when Uncle Charlie's deckchair collapses at Brid.

HOW MUCH DO WE WATCH?
On a typical day, more than three-quarters of the UK population will watch some television. Over any four-week period, about 99% of people will have seen television. The amount of time spent watching television in an average household is about six hours. For individuals, this translates into about twenty-seven hours a week - just less than four hours a day. This average does, of course, cover very wide variations in viewing habits. As might be expected, teenagers watch the least (about two and a half hours a day), whilst those over retirement age watch the most (about five hours). Income also has an affect on viewing - as a general rule, the better off you are, the less television you watch.

❧ I was reluctant to buy a video recorder. I can see the advantages of having one for 'time-shifting'. You can watch "Coronation Street" at three o'clock in the morning if you're out at 7.30, and I suppose the idea of building a library of your favourite programmes is quite appealing. When the rest of the family were getting them on interest-free credit, I wasn't tempted. Working on the principle of 'what you don't have you don't miss', I managed to resist until about six months ago. I don't know what came over me, I saw one in a sale and bought it. I can be a bit impulsive like that. I am now the proud owner of a Sharp 4 Head, double length recorder and so far have twenty five tapes which can last up to six hours because of the long play facility. Apart from "Jungle Book" which I bought at Boots, I haven't seen any of the tapes more than once and there's about seven tapes which I haven't even had a look at after taping things on them.

It was the same with the remote control 'zapper'. I refused to get one on the grounds that it would make me too lazy to get up and turn the telly over. I came home one day and was surprised to see my brother, who was lodging at the time, changing channels with a 'zapper' in hand. I asked him where he'd got it. "It's yours", he said. "How do you mean it's mine?" I couldn't understand what he was on about. "I found it on the back of your telly." I had bought our current telly about eighteen months before and apparently the remote control was attached to the back of it with a velcro fastener. I never knew all that time. This has shown me three things, my brother is too idle to turn the TV over manually, I'm too idle to dust the back of the telly, and, since I've discovered the 'zapper', I've spent more time laying on the settee than I ever did.

When it comes to using new technology, my old dad is the wonder of the age. He buys the Radio Times mid-week and cuts it up by Friday, so that every programme he wants to watch the following week is recorded on a slip of paper. By eight o'clock every morning he is up scheduling programmes. At the end of the day he pastes his notes on the front of the video tape. At night or at the end of the week he wipes what has seen. Almost everything is watched via the time warp. He slots television into his space, not the other way around. He is in control.

It is definitely not 'like father like son'. We slop down in front of the television and catch the twenty minutes of a previous programme while waiting for the one we want to see at eight o'clock and the next wholly uninteresting one which leads into our nine o'clock choice. Television in our house is for collapsing in front of.

Coin-in-the-slot television, 1957.

Enthusiast with his home-made television camera, 1950.

୬ Having done a couple of years or so in repertory, I managed eventually to get myself cast in a small character part in one episode of a television detective series called "Skyport", which was produced by a comparatively new TV company called Granada based in Deansgate, Manchester. It was then a bunch of ex-forces Nissen huts on a tidied-up bomb site. The leading man was George Moon and I played an art dealer in a tale of robbery and corruption. It was a small part, but a break-in. I was petrified as time drew near for the broadcast, for in those days the shows went out live and there was no provision for retakes. Just before we went on air, I asked a regular member of the cast what happened if I forgot my lines. He told me, almost flippantly, "If you keep moving your lips, the audience will think it's their set that's on the blink".

୬ I am an avid watcher of "Emmerdale". I live only two fields away from the village and have had several of the actors as neighbours, including Jackie Merrick and Jack Sugden, and when Fraser brought Gemma to live just across the road, I popped a card through their door wishing them much happiness and saying that I had been married at Esholt church. I felt it was a neighbourly gesture when I knew they were to be my neighbours.
I was distressed with the plane accident and was on the point of voicing my opinion at the time, but it was too late. I must say I felt it was in very bad taste, being a programme watched by people not only in the Yorkshire area and would be upsetting to friends and relatives of the Lockerbie deceased. Nevertheless I still enjoy all the local scenery and am always pleased to be able to tell people whom I meet on holidays that I live in the original farmhouse - now very much altered, which was the home of the farm manager of Esholt Hall on the Emmerdale Estate.

🍂 I fell in love with "Emmerdale Farm" at the very first programme - it was really 'me' That's because I have a great love for The Dales and West Yorkshire. This has brought me in fact, twice around the world from my home in Australia, to try to recapture the feel of the place and that bygone age that I knew in my lifetime.

I remember with pride and a tear in my eye that long time ago, when I went up to Arncliffe with my best friend from Chesterfield and became involved with the filming of Joe's wedding to Christine Sharp. What a surprise to fall on this by accident. And I remember so well my surprise at Matt, looking out of place - clean-living chap that he was, puffing his head off and leaning slovenly against the alcove, talking to Joe outside Arncliffe Church, awaiting the arrival of Christine in her carriage.

🍂 When it started, "Emmerdale Farm" was as safe and homely as your fireside rug. The family used to sit round the kitchen table as a family, tuck into bacon, egg, sausage and tomatoes and leave their wellingtons at the door. Look at it now. Aeroplanes drop on top of them, there are armed raids on the Post Office and there's more trout farming than cow milking. I preferred it as it was.

🍂 You only have to look at the opening sequences of "Emmerdale" to see how we are being manipulated and drawn away from the original spirit of the series. Today the pictures are of people hang-gliding and pony treking, whereas in the good old days it was of rolling pastures and shearing sheep. All right, so perhaps they are trying to turn us and make us accept new values, but do they have to do it so blatantly? Perhaps we would be prepared to accept Post Office raids and too-daft-to-laugh-at air crashes if they kept the old opening of sheep gamboling in meadows and people making hay.

Having said that though I am surprised by how long "Look North" has gone without modifying its up-front pictures. York Minster, Whitby, the Humber Bridge are all relevant, but why have they left it so long before getting rid of the shot of the pit head gear. Hasn't anyone told them that the coal industry has been and gone? I suppose a picture of a bulldozer extension ripping at an opencast seam doesn't quite have the same style

🍂 Arthur Scargill was made by YTV and so was Charlie Churm. Arthur was the left and Charlie was the right, so whenever the union President said anything, the lads in Kirkstall Road sent a crew down to see Mr Churm and get his views.

Charlie's office was the bar in a little pub in Hightown, Castleford, called The Black Bull, and this is where they would find him when he wasn't in the union box at Sharlston Colliery. He was outrageous and very direct. In one famous interview, when asked what would be the outcome of a particular ballot, he replied, "What ballot? Bloody hell, were they ballot papers? I've burnt them in our back garden. I wondered why the smoke was red."

🍂 I hate the soaps, I hate horse racing and I hate football on television. I used to like "Newsnight", but I hate that as well now since Jeremy Paxman joined the programme. I hate his voice, the way he gets things mixed up and his condescending attitude. In fact if he was interviewing me I'd be tempted to stick one on him. I do like the science programmes; the "Ascent of Man" was one I watched avidly. Later I bought the book by Professor Bronowski and enjoyed that and later still I had the pleasure of meeting the Professor after a lecture in Hull.

These days I use the television mainly as an information service. I come in from work, turn on the telly and then click to Ceefax. Page 367 usually gives me the motorcycle news, Page 361 or 362 is the Grand Prix. A few years ago I bought a video, but I only use it for time-shifting when I'm out. I think in all the time I've had it, I've only ever hired two films from the high street. I also have a box full of videos that I've taped and never watched. Every six or eight weeks I tape over them with something else that I don't then watch.

We don't really interact with TV do we? It is a very isolationist pursuit. They can come out with surround sound, big screen, stereo, but it's still a blooming box in the corner. No camaraderie or emotion like the pictures. I suppose interactive TV will come and that will be the day when I shall be able to stick one on Jeremy Paxman without even being interviewed by him.

TV LISTINGS

With the start of BBC TV in 1936, the Radio Times became the world's first television listings magazine. Programme details, however, only appeared in the London edition since that was the only area that could receive pictures. By 1955 all editions of the Radio Times had TV as well as radio listings and television moved from the back pages for the first time.

In 1955, with the launch of ITV, the Radio Times had a rival - TV Times. For many years these two magazines had a monopoly of weekly programme details on their respective channels. In March 1991, the listings copyright was removed and magazines were allowed for the first time to publish full details of all television programmes .

Saturday afternoons have never been the same since televised wrestling with Kent Walton and the second half of a Rugby League match with the late-great Eddie Waring vied with each other for sports viewers. Jackie Pallo was the greatest TV entertainer ever to pull on a pair of striped swimming trunks, Les Kellett was truly the Norman Wisdom of the fight game, but over on the Beeb, no finer man has ever held a bulbous microphone whilst wearing a trilby hat than Eddie "Ooop and Under" Waring. So famous he was, that he had a catchphrase. In these more sophisticated days of sports presentation, when statistics flash relentlessly at the bottom of the screen and replays rule the roost, Eddie is much maligned in Rugby circles. His quaint turn of phrase, his Northern candour, his Dewsburian wit are easy to take the mickey out of, but think about this. Have any modern Rugby commentators appeared on "It's A Knockout"? Have any of them been a guest on "Morecambe and Wise", and have any been impersonated on a regular basis by Mike Yarwood? No! Because they're boring, that's why. Eddie was colourful, a true TV personality.

Same with the wrestling, Giant Haystacks, Mick McManus and Kendo Nagasaki were larger than life entertainers, no pretentions, no qualms, no holds barred TV personalities. We should restore them to their former glory. Bring back Rugby League and wrestling on Saturday. But please, don't let them clash.

The thing about television is that it makes silly little catchphrases more memorable than the show itself, sometimes more memorable than the so-called 'personality' who says it. I can just about remember that Larry Grayson said, "Shut that door", but I can't remember what show he said it on. I can't for the life of me remember who said, "You'll wonder where the yellow went when you brush your teeth with Pepsodent", but I do remember dear Valerie Singleton saying, "Here's one that I prepared earlier".

As a small child I was always afraid of thunderstorms. Firstly, because my father was struck with lightning from a large steel bread knife which hung on the side of the pantry door. We all called this knife a 'christie'; I think it was the maker's name. Dad was flung on the kitchen floor with its force when he tried to take it down to use it.

Then, when I was aged about nine years old, we had a bad thunderstorm in our village. The farmer had four cows die, struck by lightning at the corner of his field, under some trees. We children all ran down after school to see the cows laying under the trees. So I learnt at an early age not to shelter under trees when thunder was about.

My Mother was worse than I was and always covered the mirrors over with towels. There were sheets on sideboards, dressing tables, wall mirrors and, above all, she always put the cutlery away in the drawers; specially the Christie bread knife. When television came along, that was switched off as a matter of course. The windows and doors were left open, just in case a thunderbolt came down the chimney. The theory was that the draught would take it out. I don't know if it worked, because we never had one drop in to see us.

Maureen Winner, the Radio Show Jubilee Girl, 1961.

I got married and had a child and I didn't want to pass all this on to him and frighten him. I never tried to show any unease; I never covered things up, just left the door open. Then, when my son was about four years old, he was watching the children's TV "Blue Peter" programme and Rolf Harris showed the children the sounds he could make with his 'wobble board'. After a minute or two, he asked the children what sound it was. All the children said "thunder". Later that night we had a nasty thunderstorm, but rather than being scared, my son said, "Oh, it's only Rolf with his wobble board". From that day all the fear left me and my son never was afraid at all. After thirty years I still say "Thank you Rolf Harris. You freed me from my fear".

Alexandra Palace TV mast.

CHAPTER FOUR
NEIGHBOURS

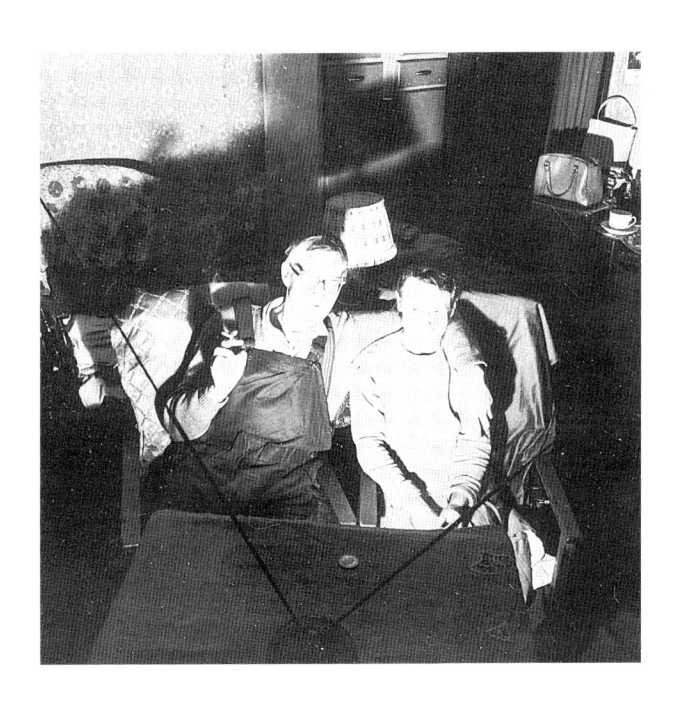

"You can watch the television if you can find it."

I detest anything that's prepacked, predigested, prescribed or processed - that's one of the reasons Des and I chose to live in a crumbling old Mendip Hill farm with an acre of land while our children were growing up. We kept chickens, grew our own vegetables, ground our wheat in a coffee mill and walked to work and school down the hill to the village. Des and I agreed on many things, but one strong point of conflict was the television; I didn't want it and he did, and so of course did the children. I was out-numbered and a small black and white portable set kept us in touch with the world.

During the wet August that we moved into Winterhead Hill Farm in 1977, Elvis Presley died and was flashed across our tiny screen in the kitchen window, wearing a white, silver-studded suit, just as the Rentokil man announced that he had found dry rot in our bathroom floorboards and began to enquire tentatively over his cup of tea. "I hope you don't mind me asking you a personal question", I pricked up my ears, " ... but what on earth makes you come and live in a place like this?".

It poured and poured outside. The roof sprang a waterfall, the ceiling in our bedroom caved in, the septic tank overflowed and the courtyard outside was awash with excrement. I must admit my heart leapt up at the sound of "Champion the Wonder Horse", and I was grateful for the inevitable posthumous Elvis films - "G I Blues", "Love Me Tender", "Jailhouse Rock", and of course "Lassie", which was on every day and kept my two and one year olds quiet while I fed the baby or baked the bread. But later on when life settled down and the children started school, TV became second only to the popping of balloons after birthday parties and the greatest source of inter-parental and inter-child conflict and irritation.

When the sitting room became habitable, the telly moved out of the kitchen. I rarely had the inclination to watch it - except for "The Thorn Birds", I guiltily admit that, and those classic serials the BBC were so good at. Des liked watching the news, but I always found this skimpy compared to the radio, but it was the time between 4.00 and 5.30 when children's television was on that caused the most trouble, rage and frustration.

The two, and later three, children would come home from school at about 4.00, snatch a hurried drink and sandwich, then make their way to the sofa where they would collapse in front of "Play School". "A house - with a door - windows - one, two, three, four - let's look through the ... arched window..." Yuk.

It's not that I object to "Play School" as such, or "Jackanory, Jackanory, Jackanory", or even "Blue Peter". It was all good, worthy, edifying, wholesome stuff - it was just that it made the children such bad company. They sat there, staring blankly, open mouthed and dumb at those silly adults who pranced around in front of them and spoke in special 'child orientated' voices, either mincing, saccharine, unremittingly enthusiastic, or slowly in words of two syllables. Not as bad a "Sesame Street" , with its hideous furry monsters which assume that children have a concentration span of two seconds and an IQ of a baboon.

ITV was mostly banned in our house , as we didn't want our children to know about things like cornflake-families and Captain Findus fish fingers, or begin to ask why our washing wasn't whiter than white. I objected to the daily after-school television habit, because it made the little blighters so unsociable and dreamy. My attempts to engage them in conversation, or mobilise them into constructive activities, or any activity for that matter, were met with indifference, a curt grunt or a monosyllabic reply.

"What did you do at school today?"

"Not much."

"Shall we go for a walk and pick blackberries before supper?"

"No, I don't want to miss "Dogtanian and the Three Muskethounds"."

"Come on Shannon, it's time to practise the piano."

"Oh no Mum, not now, it's "Dr Who"."

But worst of all, were the battles over the programmes. Their friends watched at 9.00 or 10 o'clock at night.

"Why can't I stay up to watch "An Amercian Werewolf in London"?"

"It's much too late and those films are for grown-ups and will give you nightmares."

"But mum, Robert and Dougie's mum and dad don't mind if they stay up and watch "An American Werewolf in London"..., and they don't have nightmares."

Children watching a mirror lid TV set c1938.

I hated hauling them away for family meals when some hideous hit and run American film had just started at 6.30. "Can't we have our meal in front of "Knight Rider" ? - it's so exciting."

"No." I turned off the switch violently and dragged two sullen children into the kitchen. Soon I began to resort to devious strategies to jerk them out of their torpor. I removed the fuse from the plug and told them disingenuously, "Sorry, the telly's packed up". It was surprising how quickly they got used to the silence. The 'Lego' came out again, they would crowd around the kitchen table to draw or play the memory game, or just disappear outside if it was fine. The house seemed much more peaceful now that the intruder was quiet and the children were free to be themselves. It didn't last for long though.

"When are you going to fix the telly?"

Dad fixed it for them after a week because he wanted to watch it, and I was back then gnashing my teeth again. This was a typical broken-record argument between us:

Me: "They were perfectly happy without it, it stifles their imagination and turns them into couch potatoes."

Des: "Don't be ridiculous, they only watch it a couple of hours a day. Anyway, you can't isolate them completely, we're already three miles away from the village. Besides, it's up to you how much they watch, you can control it."

"That's all very well in theory, but you're not the one who has to drag them off to their music practises, or argue with them everytime you switch it off, nor do you have to pull them apart when they fight over which programme to watch ..."

"You've got to be realistic, all their friends watch it - they're going to feel complete outsiders if they can't join in with conversations at school."

"I don't care if they're different - I want them to have minds of their own ... Blah, Blah, Blah."

My loathing of the little white box grew into an obsession as the children's demands for TV watching increased. I hated myself when I gave way to them and was racked with guilt if I used it as a babysitter. There were times when I felt tempted to kick in the screen. I felt it was the enemy gnawing away at their imagination and playtime - bringing unwanted people and bland programmes into the house, destroying our privacy and individuality. I wondered if 'Jane Eyre' or 'Wuthering Heights' would ever have been written if the Bronte children had watched "Playschool" or "Jackanory". Would Shakespeare have bothered to write any plays at all if he had spent his afternoons and evenings staring at a screen instead of wandering about the Warwickshire fields or joking and playing with his friends?

I suspect tomorrow's children won't even know what a real daffodil or primrose looks like - not one you can touch or feel, only its flickering facsimile on a screen. How dismal to think that children should prefer the passive torpor of adventure on the screen to the excitement of dressing up and making up stories, playing hide and seek with friends, making dens in the woods or scrumping apples. I swore that this should not be my children's fate - but how could I avoid it?

At last I found the perfect compromise. When I got really sick of the thing, I picked up the telly and hid it under a pile of old towels and clothes in the airing cupboard, then smugly carried on weeding the onions to the sound of the afternoon play on the radio. When the children came home from school, there was a stunned silence when they noticed the empty space in the sitting room. "Where's the telly mum, it's "Grange Hill" today", came the dismayed voices. I continued hoeing the onions and replied blithely, "I've hidden it - you can watch the television if you can find it".

Stina Harris

☙ It always strikes me as a bit strange. The world is filled with geriatric patients who have been sitting there without a visitor for weeks on end and the reason why no one is coming to see them at 6.30 visiting is that the relatives don't like to turn out because an Australian Soap is on the telly: "Neighbours. Everybody needs good neighbours".

☙ She was obviously distressed, lonely, approaching middle age. He had gone off somewhere, not with anyone in particular; she admitted that. "Where did we go wrong?" was what she said, "Everything was so normal, we would sit in front of the fire together every Sunday evening, eating buttered scones and watching "The Golden Shot".

ଌ To watch "Come Dancing" in colour had been Gran's ultimate ambition over since the invention of colour TV. It was to be many years before she would be able to afford her own set, but her older sister, Laura, got one shortly after they came out. Great Aunt Laura had married a man who worked in insurance. They lived in a bungalow and had seven sorts of buns on the cake stand at Sunday teatime. They were what might be termed, the well-to-do side of the family.

For some reason, "Come Dancing" was always and probably still is shown very late at night. It never occurred to Gran then, that she could visit sister Laura, who lived about a mile away, stay late to watch her programme and then walk home in the dark as the pubs and clubs were turning out. Then one day, Grandad said that if Gran wanted she should stay at Laura's, watch "Come Dancing" and that he would pick her up when the club chucked out. She tried it and came home gushing with tales about hand-sewn sequins, chiffon sleeves and polka-dotted polka dancers. After that it became a weekly ritual, Grandad would accompany Gran to Aunt Laura's bungalow, return to the Coronation Working Men's Club for a few jars and a game of dominoes, then soft-shoe shuffle his way back to pick up Gran at midnight.

Now when I think about it, I think about a couple in a romantic setting. Gran doing the Palais Glide in the moonlight back home, linking Grandad's arm as he breathed a beery mist into the cold night air. And I fantasise about what they might have talked about, Gran dreaming of sequins on beautiful dresses, Grandad thinking about the spots on his dominoes.

ଌ There was only one person on our part of the street had a television and several families gathered there to watch. The neighbour, Mrs Hughes, spent her day making cups of tea for us all in between watching. Then, around 1959, my husband and I, who were only courting at that time, lived a hundred miles apart. We relied on television to bring us together. Although we were apart, we decided to watch "Wagon Train", which was on at both places at the same time, so we could be together in spirit.

WHAT DO WE WATCH?

Since the 1980s, viewers have been presented with an increasing amount of choice. As well as the start of Channel 4, there has been the growth of cable and satellite television. The number of hours broadcast has also increased dramatically due to the filling in of time that was previously the jealous preserve of the test card. We now have daytime television, breakfast television and late-night television. The amount of time that we spend viewing, however, has not increased. So, what do we choose to watch?

ITV has the greatest audience share - 40%. BBC1 has 33%, BBC2, 10% and Channel 4, 11%. At the moment, satellite and cable account for just 6% of all television viewing. When we consider the different types of programmes shown the audience share is:

Drama - 24%
Light Entertainment - 20%
News and Current Affairs - 20%
Feature Films - 12%
Childrens TV - 6%
Documentaries - 8%
Sport - 8%
Music and Arts - 1%
Religious - 1%

In 1993, the last year for which figures are available, the most popular programme was Coronation Street, with some episodes attracting an audience of over twenty million.

❧ We set up the 'Television Heaven' section of the National Museum only last year. You come, pick a programme and then retire to a booth to watch it. Most of the booths are open and passers-by can watch as you wander through looking at the sixth episode of "Coronation Street" or the first one of Trevor Griffiths' "Bill Brand", eyes glued to the screen, large earphones on your head.

Most of the viewers seem to last no more than ten minutes, but there are a few dedicated individuals who come back week after week and spend hours here. They are the serious students of television who want to see more than the first "Spitting Image" or "Johnny Cash in San Quentin Prison".

Everything is controlled from a monitoring section. Two of us introduce the viewers to the scheme and then when a choice is made, ensure that everything runs smoothly. One of the five viewing areas however is different. This is a larger enclosed room. The seats are round the wall and there is the facility for freezing a frame or moving backwards and forwards. Lights can be up full or down low. When you think of it, this is the nearest a visitor gets to the old fashioned cinema. In this room it is possible to sit in the dark with strangers.

The other facility it has is that it can function like the back row of the cinema and it does. Occasionally courting couples, often Asian boys and girls, retire there for a bit of gentle snogging. Of course, all can be viewed on the small monitoring screen because there is a camera in the corner, but I prefer to let life move forward; not watching, not intervening.

TV Heaven at the National Museum of Photography, Film, & Television.

🞂 In those days they called it, "Going the whole way", and although people will talk to you about the way they courted in the back row, and although I am sure that a minority lost their virginity there, television provided more opportunities than are generally admitted. The suggestion that we would like to watch the end of a late night show provided me and my girlfriend with a reason to stay up after my parents had gone to bed. Television legitimised the opportunity for courting inside the house and put it into an appropriate time frame, one which was agreed by all interested parties.

"You don't mind, Mr and Mrs Sylvester, if we stay up to watch 'Whicker's World'?"

"No, love. It's of no interest to us, but you stay up."

We did. Irene was down to her Maidenform bra and me in my Y-fronts before Mom's bedroom door closed.

🞂 My husband's mother was very prim and proper and sex was completely taboo. Even her husband had never seen her undressed. She'd put her nightie on with the lights out before getting into bed; that was throughout all her married life. I suppose she was sexually-repressed. But she used to watch the wrestling on telly and you should have seen her then. She used to get really sexually excited watching Big Daddy.

🞂 Many odd things go on in television studio centres that viewers would never dream of. Normally, late shifts are not very popular with staff. This occasion, however, was an exception. It happened in 1961 or '62. From the transmission area it was possible to look out of the window and across the street, into the bedroom of a flat on the other side of the road. There was a young lady who lived there with her father. On Friday nights he went out for a drink. Anyway, that was what we supposed because every Friday night she would be joined in the flat by her boyfriend. They had a regular schedule and could always be seen 'getting down to business' on the rug in front of the fire.

More often than not, they would turn off the light in the room. They did, however, leave the television switched on and, by the light of its glow the proceedings could still be observed by all the telecine and videotape engineers who were peering through the window opposite. The timing of this evening's diversion coincided with the showing of the late-night film on ATV and, as often as not, this was the programme the couple were watching (or probably not watching very much). This could be proved scientifically by lifting the black level of the film being transmitted. Gradually, the engineers would raise the black level in an attempt to make the TV screen brighter and hence get a better view of the room. They had to be quite careful when they did this. The equipment in the Post Office circuits between the studios and the transmitter didn't like the increased level and would occasionally drop out, causing all the screens in the region to go blank!

🞂 They'll all be sitting round following the nine o'clock watershed, watching a play or something. Gran in the Shackleton chair, Mom on the settee with a box of Quality Street and Dad in the uncomfortable one by the glass topped table, when a couple who we had seen earlier in an Edwardian dining hall suddenly appear in the buff and start rolling about. Gran seems to take it in her stride, watching as she completes the crossword puzzle book. Dad has more problems and starts a conversation about whether Everton will win the Cup this year or not. This produces a reaction in Mom, "Shut up", she says sharply, "I'm trying to watch sex on television."

🞂 Most people would remember film and variety shows from way back, but I remember the wonderous expression on my small daughter's face when she saw the first commercials, two of her favourites being, "Beanz Meanz Heinz" and "Andrews Salts". Although only three years old, she picked up all the jingles quickly.

Everyone loved the adverts then. And of course there was "Andy Pandy" and "Bill and Ben", which was a ritual for the little ones; mine would settle down to watch after dinner ages before they were due on.

Our daughter could not pronounce 'effervescing'. Once, on a bus, she suddenly piped up, "Andrews! Andrews! effing, effing Andrews!. All the passengers turned to look, then all burst out laughing. She didn't know why.

COMMERCIALS

Television advertising began in Britain on 22 September 1955 with the start of ITV. ITV's critics claimed that the service would be too American and that the British public would not accept having their programmes interrupted by adverts.

The first commercial broadcast was for Gibbs SR toothpaste. It featured a tube of toothpaste set inside a block of ice. The commentary told viewers about its 'tingling fresh' qualities. The morning after the first adverts were shown Bernard Levin wrote in the *Manchester Guardian* 'I feel neither depraved nor uplifted by what I have seen...certainly the advertising has been entirely innocuous. I have already forgotten the name of the toothpaste.'

Television advertising has come a long way since 1955. Many products have disappeared and been replaced by others, undreamt of forty years ago. However, classic adverts of the past live on in viewers' memories. So too do their slogans - 'The Esso sign means happy motoring', 'Beanz meanz Heinz' and many, many others.

Today, television advertising is worth over £2,600 million each year. Much more than the income which the BBC receives through the licence fee.

⁂ They wanted an audience for the television presentation of Tony Harrison's 'V'. I'm never that keen about being on television, but this was an exception. Harrison is, in my opinion, one of the greatest poets we have produced in the last two centuries and this was one of his major works. I guessed that the idea of presenting it as a straight poem would run into controversy and I was proved right. The schedules were announced and, in their traditional manner, Tory MPs rose in the House of Commons to condemn a work that they had heard about but not read.

'Strong language shouldn't be heard at all - and definitely not before milkmen went to bed'. That was the message. They succeeded in pushing the programme later and later into the night. Eventually it went out at 10.30pm. I watched the programme with some apprehension, scared that the producer would not let the words speak for themselves. It's not often that a producer is prepared to keep the camera on a standing figure but this one, to his credit, did. Occasionally, though, the camera did wander across the faces of the audience. That is where I became useful. There were close-ups and general views and then, when one particular word that was likely to give offence came up, a soft-focus, full-faced picture of me. I appeared safe and respectable, you see. What could possibly be wrong with the world if a scholarly, middle-aged gentleman could take in such filth with apparent equanimity?

⁂ If the sun came out the picture disappeared. So dad bought one of the dark screens to put over the TV screen, like a pair of sunglasses. We were watching a programme one evening and it showed the sperm meeting the egg and dividing. Just as it was on my brother walked through the room, glanced at the TV and, still on the move, said, "What's that?"
Quick as a flash a very embarrassed mom said, "They're making cheese".
He replied, "I arn't eating cheese any more!"

❧ My dad is a surgeon and a few years ago he got asked to take part in this film for "Rainbow" about children going into hospital. As I waited with my friends at playschool, I can remember feeling a bit mixed up. On the one hand I was proud - not everybody's dad gets on television - but at the same time I was embarrassed and wanted him to be like everybody else's dad and not be there at all.

I shouldn't have worried, because although they had three crews of eight working for three shifts, the resultant bit of film was very, very short. All they showed of dad was a clipping of him dressed for an operation and the lines, "Dr Thingermy is wearing 'special' clothes - sterilised clothes".

We still use that as a family saying. The effect is made by putting extraordinary emphasis on the word 'special'.

❧ The accents have changed over the years, but then so has the language. When the advertisements first came on there were always two precisely dressed women talking about washing-up liquid, soap powder or toothpaste. Since Northerners were by definition uncouth and scruffy, there was clearly an educational process going on and in a big way. We were asked to wonder, especially, "Where the yellow went when we brushed our teeth with Pepsodent", and what happened to the understains when we tried Persil. I was impressed and continue to ask, if Pepsodent was so vital, why isn't it around any more and why the charming euphemism 'understain' is neither a part of current language or has been replaced? And while you are at it is denture plaque a real word?

❧ "Bewitched" was my daughter's favourite programme. She was most annoyed when they took it of. She stamped her feet and told me to magic it on again by rubbing my nose. My son loved to get dressed up in his uniform with IR on his little hat, to watch "Thunderbirds - International Rescue". Some years later I had to buy a colour TV for him and his cousin to watch the Cup Final, so they could see the blood on the footballers' shins - little horrors!

❧ We never had television in our house until about 1973. I can remember one of my cousins visiting us and bringing her four year old son. As soon as they got in the house, the little lad looked round the room, put his hands on his hips and asked, "Where's the telly?". When we said we hadn't got one, he pulled a face and said, "What can we do then?". My sister and I soon showed him plenty of games and things. When it came to home time, he didn't want to leave.

❧ There's no telly before school in the morning, no telly before homework and no telly after 8.30 at night. We sometimes watch it while we have our tea, but mum doesn't like that. We haven't got Sky. When they talk about programmes on Sky and cable at school, I just keep quiet. We've had that argument at home already.

❧ We were very proud of our toddler son who was absolutely fascinated by the stranger in our living room and refused to leave it alone, fingering and prodding, poking and banging it, in an effort to make it come to life with pictures.

Short of parting with the TV set, or parting with our son, we had to do something. So I found a large strong cardboard box which fitted snuggly over the entire TV set and I painted a screen complete with controls and knobs on the outside of the box. I then pushed some real knobs from an old radio set into the cardboard so that our son could fiddle to his hearts content. After he had gone to bed we could remove the cover and watch our favourites like "Coronation Street" and "Criss Cross Quiz" in peace and comfort.

In an ideal world, children's eyes should be opened to as many kinds of activity and entertainment as possible. Making robots out of yoghurt pots, playing musical instruments, reading, making gingerbread men, putting on plays and so on is not enough. These days, a rounded childhood must include computer games and telly as well. It's the excessive watching of telly that's the problem, not the telly itself. Indeed, it's the excessive doing of anything. If a child were forced to go out camping and morris dancing every single weekend of his life, for instance, and never given a chance to do anything else, his childhood would be just as limited as if he spent each weekend glued to the box.

Television can be addictive and controlling an addiction is not easy. You should set an example to your children and aim to make the telly a guest in your home rather than the master of it.

A portable so light that a child can carry it.
The KB "Featherlight" transistor TV, 1964.

One way of clipping television's wings is to get a video and make it a rule that nothing is watched until it has been recorded, even if it's striaght after it has been on. It's a fantastic fag to have to set the video recorder and requires a positive effort; also, for some unknown reason, it's not quite as much fun watching recorded programmes as ones fresh off the screen. It's quite easy to bar the telly from breakfast, lunch and supper. It isn't a member of the family, after all; it's a mere lodger and has no place laid at the dining table. You don't have to have a set of written rules, just a set of agreed deadlines that will keep the telly in its place.

Some people can have just the occasional cigarette after a meal; others smoke forty a day. Some people only have a cream bun as a treat; while others can't stop stuffing their faces. If, through your own example, you can teach your children to stay in control of their entertainments, you will have taught them a lesson far more important than anything they can learn from books, creative play or, indeed, TV itself.

❧ Aged around thirteen or fourteen, I befriended a girl who became of advantage to me in my teenage years. Amanda's Dad owned our local video shop and was not particular about the types of films he allowed us to borrow. Suffering from the typical teenage condition of doing everything I was supposed not to do, I would borrow videos of both fifteen and eighteen certificate that were considered unsuitable for my age. Titles such as the "Exorcist", "Robocop" and the "Terminator" gave us street cred in the playground and allowed us to participate in the bragging games that went on. If you hadn't seen "Nightmare On Elm Street" you were considered quite 'uncool'. Yet I seem to remember that although I had seen many of the films that my peers regarded as the 'hard' thing to watch, I really wasn't very cool at all. What my friends didn't know was that I probably saw very little of the film at all, as I would spend all the time hiding behind a cushion, just as I used to do as a child watching "Dr Who", and as I still do today if anything slightly scary or violent comes on the telly.

❧ A few months ago, whilst watching a holiday programme, a number flashed up for viewers to ring if they wished to enter a competition to win a trip to the Bahamas for four people. All you had to do was answer a simple question, like. 'Which cartoon character eats spinach?' I knew the answer, of course, and stupidly thought that nobody else would know that Popeye was our man. I proceeded to ring the number again and again as there were no restrictions on how many times you rang in. I also got three friends to call in so as to increase our chances of winning. I didn't win and neither did my friends but we did manage to spend about a hundred pounds between us ringing up the 48p per minute phone line that conveniently keeps you on the line for about four minutes each time. Admittedly, this money might not have paid for an exotic holiday, but we could all have had a day out in Blackpool, a game of bingo and still had enough left for a fish and chip supper.

❧ My son was born prematurely and because of that he always had a bit of a problem in co-ordination and learning and reading. But he adored television; he lived for it and still does. We tried to stop him watching television by not telling him what was on, so he taught himself to read by reading the TV and Radio Times so that he would know what was on. By the time he went to school, he could read quite well. Now he's got 'Sky' and just watches television all the time.

❧ My ninety-four year old auntie, Ida Walker, worked for forty years in our town of Hemsworth, as a nurse in the Southmoor hospital, then as Relief District Nurse and then retiring as a doctor's surgery nurse. It's this last job that brought her to watch children's television programmes, such as "The Woodentops", "Andy Pandy" and "The Flower Pot Men".

One day when she went to work, one of the doctors said to her, "Nurse, why is it you don't have the children crying when you inject them?"

She replied to a very impressed doctor, "It's because I watch TV children's programmes.
He said, "Don't tell me you watch them".
"Yes doctor, I do, when I'm doing my housework. Because when I've seen "Andy Pandy, or "The Woodentops", or "The Flower Pot Men", and the children come for their injections, I always say the opposite to what has been shown on the TV. The children then argue with me and by the time they've told me about what happened, I've injected them and they don't know they've had the needle."

*Trendy decor. Sanderson "Naivete" wallpaper, 1969.
Bright pink flowers on a dark green background.*

🙦 I have had my pet rabbits for a lot less time than I've had my black and white television. Even so, they have names - Bimbo and Trevor - whereas my set, which travels around with me and has been in my rooms in Brighton, Ealing and Didsbury, remains nameless. I think that is really sad, especially when you think that he is at least twelve years old - four years older than I was when dad bought him for me.

A twelve year old dog would be about seventy-two in human terms, so it stands to reason that a television of that age in a consumer-durable society has got to be nudging a hundred. If he was human he would be just about ready for a telegram from the Queen by now, and yet I can't even remember his make. It's a wonder that that he switches on at all. Yet he does, although not without some misgivings. He will only perform if you give him a little slap on an exact spot on the top of his left hand side. Of course, you have to move the vase of flowers and the photographs beforehand.

> **WHAT'S YOURS CALLED?**
> C P Scott of the Manchester Guardian, is reputed to have said : 'Television? No good will come of this device. The word is half Greek and half Latin.' (*Tele* - Greek = Far, *Visio* - Latin = Sight) When TV arrived, people soon adopted other, friendlier, names for the new box in their homes.
>
> The use of the term *set* as a general name for a piece of electrical equipment dates back to the last century. People often referred to their wireless as *the set* and this usage soon transfered to television. Similarly, *the box* was often used to describe a gramophone or wireless. People soon began to speak of their TV set as *the box*.
>
> Shortening names is a sure sign of affection. Hence the widespread use of *the telly*. Not all terms, however, are affectionate. Critics have come up with *the idiots' lantern, the goggle-box* and *the boob tube*.

🙦 The very first time I saw a TV was at a friend's home. It was so far up the wall we got neck-ache watching it. I'd be about nine years old at the time. I later found out the reason for this. It was such a new piece of furniture that my friend's dad who was very strict and had seven children said that no of them were allowed to touch it. I was amazed when I went into other friends' houses and saw TVs at a reasonable level. I thought all televisions were put halfway up the wall.

🙦 In about 1976 "Emmerdale" came to Appleby Bridge to film a Jubilee Street Party and, as one of the young kids from the neighbourhood, I crowded down to see what was going off. Most were paid actors, but they let me into a crowd scene and my family and friends saw me on television. It was that that turned me on and here I am twenty years later lugging a camera around for "Calendar". Mind you, I was an actor when I was eleven. Never again!

🙦 British advertisements are so well in advance of what you see in Hong Kong and Singapore, that sometimes I watch them for fun. You remember the British product because the advertisement is witty and subtle, whereas in the Far East you are told no more than, "This product is expensive and it is good". They're not going to advertise something as low cost as 'Warburtons bread', it's all diamond action wrist watches, or else it's 'Tiger Beer' sold by scantily dressed girls on beaches with men in suits.

The other thing you notice about Singapore is the censorship. It is a very safe, very ordered society, with little or no crime. This is achieved by blotting out anything of which the government disapproves. Every night at 9.30 they show a movie, but when there is any violence or sex, the screen just goes blank. Everything goes - the image, the sound, the incidental music. Even if the tension of the piece is controlled by that particular scene, it is wiped off the screen.

Hong Kong television is not censored in this way and, instead of having one nightly movie, they have two and probably more 'Tiger Beer'.

✒ The first advert for "Access" showed men in the sort of open-necked shirts and bell bottoms which now I associate with 'Sally Army' hostels. It was slick for 1975, but looks a bit comical today.

However, there is one feature which does hold its own and that is the slogan; it said, "Access - take the waiting out of wanting". During the Toxteth Riots in the early 1980s this was slightly modified and graffittied onto a Liverpool wall; 'Access' in the original was replaced with the word 'Looting'.

✒ I cannot stand seeing dead people on television. It's not because they often look grotesque because they have been killed in violent situations, or starved to death - though that is always upsetting - my problem is that the act of showing them to us as we sit in front of sets with a full tray on our knee causes them to seem undignified; we see them as they would not wish to be viewed.

✒ The telephone rang just after four. It was my Dad, calling from Birmingham. 'Where's John? He said.
'Liverpool, I expect. Why?'
He didn't answer but asked another question.
'He's not gone to the match, then?'
'What match?'
'You haven't been watching the television, have you?'
'No'.
That was how I heard about the Hillsborough disaster. My Dad, down in Birmingham, watching his television, had realised that his grandson, actually an Everton fan, might just have travelled to Sheffield to see the match. Worried, he had telephoned me to share his fears. I immediately got on the phone. John was safe but deeply shocked. He had bought a few cans and settled down to enjoy the game but instead had watched the horror unfold. Television had united our family in sadness.

Television graveyard.
Scrap-dealer Alfred Padgett, restorer of old TV sets, 1967.

❧ I have vivid pictures in my mind of how I said prayers for the starving childen of Biafra at Junior School assembly every morning. These pictures have stayed with me for twenty five years; children with extended bellies and flies in the corners of their eyes. I suppose Biafra was the first time a major disaster from a developing nation had been brought to our living rooms. The first time we asked, "How come they can get television cameras there but not bread ?".

Since then of course we've had the horrors of the Vietnam War, the Ethiopian famine, the football stadium disasters at Heysel and Bradford and CNN TV bringing us the Gulf War like it was a hi-tech arcade game. Why are we fascinated by disasters, have we become so immune to seeing those pictures that we don't really believe it's true? I remember watching that fire at Bradford and listening to John Helm's very dignified commentary and thinking I must turn it off, but I didn't. The same with Heysel, the TV pictures and dead and dying seemed to roll for hours and I sat and watched in awful fascination. There is something quite absurd, something perverse about it surely, or is it that the TV pictures don't give us the real picture? Perhaps they're saying disasters only happen elsewhere and not to you.

❧ I had settled in front of the television in my house in Maine to watch a key match in the World Cup series, when the newscaster announced that the ex-American football star and television personality, O J Simpson, sought in connection with the murder of his wife and her lover, was driving along a freeway in L.A. followed by a posse of police cars and holding a gun to his temple. Within minutes, a small rectangle showing a line of cars appeared in the top right hand corner of the screen. The television helicopter clearly was on course, though really there was little to see. Once, I thought I could pick out a hand holding a gun, but maybe I only saw it because the reporter said that that was what I should see.

After sometime, the pictures reversed. The World Cup match now appeared in the corner of the screen and the main image was the cars. Eventually, the World Cup disappeared altogether and we just had the score relayed to us courtesy of some soap manufacturer or other.

❧ Whilst ostensibly selling whiter-than-white washing powder to housewives, television advertisers provided a signal for the less than pure amongst us. As an acronym it had its uses. It is said that the lonely housewives of Hull used to signal to lovers by placing a packet of this washing powder on the kitchen windowsill - "Old Man Out".

Language changes. Would anyone today think of naming a washing powder "OMO"?

❧ Although I think of television mainly as a vehicle for peddling smut, I do like a good cloak-and-dagger. So I was pleased to be watching the La Carré film on television. When it came to an end though, I was wild. I went over and phoned the television company at once. It's always a good idea to have the number to hand. "Excuse me", I said to the girl on the other end of the line, "but in the film that has just finished, you say that it was filmed on location in London, Athens and Tokyo and in the Pinewood Studios. Well, there is no way it could have been filmed in Japan because the cars drive on the opposite side of the road". She didn't seem to understand what I was talking about.

"And while I'm at it, there was a clicking throughout the programme, I think that you might have got the reel on the wrong way."

❧ My brother watches the advertisements and then writes off letters of complaint. On his fortieth birthday he sent a letter saying that, although the bottles on television give a satisfying 'pop' when opened, three out of the forty he had ordered for the occasion made no noise at all. The company replied that he should understand the special feature which had been devised to create the 'pop'. It was made by the air which is trapped between the top of the beer and the cap. Absence of the 'pop' means that there is more beer then usual in the bottle and the three guests who did not hear the 'pop' were in fact in receipt of more beer. For that reason they could not refund his money.

Currently, he is awaiting a reply from Cadburys about the size of the nuts in his chocolate compared with those seen on the screen.

🌺 I've complained twice to television. The first time was when that murderer kidnapped a girl and put her down a shaft in Staffordshire. They stated that he had a sixteen year old daughter and mentioned her by name. I argued that it was bad enough having a father who behaved in that way, without having your name going out through millions of television sets.

The next time was about fifteen years later. A nurse over Grantham way had murdered a number of children. The local news programme which reported the end of the trial, started off with a nurse in close-up, the light behind her, preparing a syringe and went on to a shot in which she approached, again in silhouette, through swing doors. It was sensational and especially insensitive if seen by those involved in the case, or those with young children ready to go into hospital. I phoned as quickly as I could and, although it was no longer than a quarter of an hour after the programme finished, I got an answerphone. This incensed me. Believing that I was not going to get anywhere, I dashed off a letter and sent it to my MP asking for details of how many complaints were logged. I did this because I didn't want an anodine letter thanking me for my concern and wishing me a Happy Christmas. Well over a hundred people had complained.

🌺 This man walks into a restaurant and is approached by the waiter, named Gervaise. The man says. 'Can I have some squid , please?' Gervaise then takes him over to the fish tank and says 'I'm sorry Sir, but we have only got a small, light green one with a hairy lip.' The man says that he doesn't mind. So Gervaise takes the squid out of the tank and carries it into the kitchen. Just as he is about to cut him up, the squid says 'No! No!' This upsets Gervaise, so he asks Hans, the dish washer, to help him. Hans is just about to chop up the squid when it again shouts out. 'No! No!' Hans breaks down in tears, sobbing 'I can't do this'. This goes to show that Hans that does dishes is as soft as Gervaise with mild green hairy-lipped squid.

🌺 Adverts have definitely had an effect on youth culture. I heard this joke during the 1960s. A teacher asks her class, "Can anyone give me a sentence including the word 'judicious'?"
"Yes Miss", shouts little Tommy, sitting bolt upright, "For hands that judicious feel as soft as your face".

Mr and Mrs Harrison and their thirty-year-old TV set, 1968.

🍂 When children go on coach trips they don't sing sexist classics, like "Silver Dollar", lewd songs such as "Ive Got A Lovely Bunch of Coconuts", or spirited oldies such as "Daisy, Daisy" any more. Instead, they sing television jingles - "If you like a lot of chocolate on your biscuit join our Club", and `Opal fruits. Made to make your mouth water.'

I know that this can be traced back to songs like, "We are the Ovaltinies, Little girls and boys", but now we have a deluge and that is sad. There's more to life than sex and shopping.

🍂 This story is more than likely apocryphal, but worth telling none the less.

A young teacher of Religious Education at a school in Harrogate wanted to explain to her class about Saul's conversion on he road to Damascus. She asked the question, "Right children. Put your hands up if you can tell me something about Damascus". Straightaway young Billy shoots his hand high into the air and says, "Please Miss, it kills 95% of all known germs".

The first coach to be fitted with television, 1967.

🕭 The great black and white children's TV series, "William Tell", starring Conrad Phillips fighting weekly battles with the Hamburger Gessler, had perhaps one of the most memorable theme tunes. If my memory serves me right, it went something like this:

"Come away, come away with William Tell
Come away, from a land he loved so well
On the day, on the day when the apple fell
For Tell and Switz - er - land
Come away, come away from the mountain side
Look down to the pass where the tyrants ride
Send a bolt, send a bolt and down they fell
For Tell and Switz - er - land
Hurry on, hurry on, there's a pungent smell
Hurry on, hurry on, there's a noose as well
But he'll escape from the jaws of hell
For Tell and Switz - er - land."

At our junior school we used to gallop up and down the playground slapping our own backsides, then shooting imaginary apples off the dinner ladies' heads. And we would sing:

"Come away, come away with William Tell
Stick a fork up his arse and he'll run like hell."

Popeye had a similar effect. We corrupted the words of the Popeye tune to:

"I'm Popeye the sailorman
I live in a caravan
I went to the pictures, without any britches
I'm Popeye the sailorman."

🕭 One sure way of sorting out the middle class from the rest was to ask an adult what Michelangelo, Raphael, Leonardo and Donatello had in common. If they replied that they were all Florentine artists their class background was obvious. Every working class person realised that they were cartoon turtles. Of course, there was no such division amongst children. Every child - whether working, middle or upper class knew who they were. I found this out in Scunthorpe when I went to a toy shop, clutching a piece of paper carrying these four names.

🕭 My earliest memory of watching television was watching the moon landings. I was seven or eight years old. My dad made us go to bed early, so that he could get us up again late at night or early in the morning to watch it. We had mugs of cocoa and I suppose we had school the next day. It was an old black and white telly, but those pictures really stick in my mind. I suppose all little boys are interested in space travel, but ever since then that's all I've really enjoyed watching - "Star Trek", "Horizon", programmes about science. That sort of thing.

🕭 Television was going to solve everything. Although I came from a somewhat cynical family - my dad said that its coming would mean that you would not only hear the gramophone record, but also see the man putting it on. As a schoolteacher, I really believed that my potential repetoire of teaching aids would expand as soon as television came into its own. It didn't in the secondary school, though it might have done in the juniors, for there you were not restricted by timetables and twenty five minute changes of lesson.

🞂 Ted was perhaps best known for his ability to pick and place money on horses that never won. Others thought of him as the finest 'ripper' to have worked at Sharlston Pit, while some recalled his ability with the right hook. I have one vivid image of him. It is a tea-time television image.

He is sitting in his favourite chair and puffing on a pipe. Bamber Gascoigne recites his catchphrase, "And now Queens, your starter for ten is .... Where are the Islets of Langerhans situated?". A long-haired man in a tie-dyed shirt presses a buzzer and his name lights up. He is usually called 'de Montfort' and has previously introduced himself as someone who is reading jurisprudence. He stutters slightly, then says, "Are they in the Outer Hebrides?" Bamber rejoins, "Wrong. Five point penalty to Queens, the question goes over to Magdalen College." At which point Ted bangs his head on the armchair, as though pressing his own imaginary button and shouts, "Ha! Any silly bugger knows the islets of Langerhans are in the pancreas. In the bloody Hebrides? Ha!"

And of course Ted is right. He nearly always was. In years of avidly watching "University Challenge", whistling its theme tune and making sure he'd got his pint of tea and Wednesday night mussels down before it started, he rarely was beaten to the buzzer by Oxbridge's finest.
Ted worked at the pit for forty years. He had a little engraved brass lamp to prove it. His formal education had finished at thirteen, when he became a pit pony driver. Yet what he didn't know about human biology, choral music, political history and yes, throw in jurisprudence, only Bamber Gascoigne knows.

🞂 You could tell the seriousness of a situation by what happened to the television. If neighbours dropped in, then the volume remained as it was, or got turned up by dad if he didn't like the person visiting. Our dad used television in a way it wasn't written about in the advertisements. If strangers - the insurance man, a new boyfriend or a teacher - came in, it got turned down. It went completely silent if the priest or doctor, or somebody in authority visited us. Mam might even turn the set right off if there was a death in the immediate family, or an operation in which they 'took everything away'.

🞂 Christmas was never the same after dad died. Mum kept up the tradition of inviting dad's unmarried brother and sister to stay, but eventually we made more of a celebration at New Year. We were invited to visit another auntie and uncle who lived a few streets away. They had a television. We didn't. Uncle used to like Jimmy Shand and his band and watched all the Scottish TV programmes to see the New Year in. We even got to have a drop of sherry - something else we never had in our house, to toast the New Year.

🞂 When I first moved to London as a student, I rented a couple of rooms at the top of a big old house. The landlady lived on the premises. She'd run it as a kind of nursing home before this latest business. Large shelves in the bathroom were full of ceramic bed-pans, urine bottles and various other strange appliances related to this former life. Two other people rented rooms. One was always referred to as 'doctor' - I don't believe he was medical, but a doctor of something at a university. The other, a young woman, was, I think, a secretary with boyfriend trouble - she looked like Kathy Kirby. I hardly ever saw these other two residents.
I got very lonely and homesick living there, but my landlady said I could always go down and watch TV with her and two of her friends. I did so most evenings for that first year, though how I stuck it I'll never know - three old ladies and me huddled in her tiny bedsit room, watching black and white TV. My landlady smoked like a chimney and created quite a thick smog during each evening's viewing. She used to say she hoped colour TV would come in before she died; she wanted to see the Queen in colour .

Is anybody there? Waiting for Wimbledon, 1937.

❧ When Jack Hulme, the Fryston photographer, got old and ill, he hit on an original idea for exercising the dog. Jack had always been one for gadgets, so the video recorder was just that; a new toy to be used in an unusual way. He had noticed that the dog had a tendency to jump for the ball whenever it appeared. He utilised this observation, recorded a Wigan versus Castleford game, and put it on whenever the dog seemed to want to go out. He would also entertain guests with this phenomena, but for me it was always disconcerting to have a dog trampolining about, as Martin Offiah rushed for touch and you tried to weedle from Jack more about the methods of creating pictures on an enlarger made from a vacuum cleaner.

🍀 When I was born, just like all my brothers and sisters, the first thing that my Grandfather ever bought me was a Manchester United scarf. For my fourth birthday, he took me to see my first game and, for my sixth birthday, he got me junior club membership. My Grandad lived and breathed football. For him, Manchester United was a religion and his passion rubbed off on me. However, in recent years football has become a very expensive business with tickets becoming very expensive and difficult to get hold off. Even if you are lucky enough to come by a ticket, more often than not you will be sitting so high up in the stand that you can hardly see the game.

However, this has now all changed. I can now have a superb view of the game as well as the bonus of a comfy seat and instant action replay. Yes, Sky Sport's football coverage has been the answer to my prayers. If only Grandad were still alive to enjoy the benefit. Although the initial expense of buying or renting the dish and paying the subscription is a little costly, it is still peanuts when you consider what you would have to pay travelling to and getting tickets for all the matches. Some cynics would argue that you lose all the atmosphere watching a game on television. All I can say is that they should come around to my house on a Sunday afternoon when twenty of us are squeezed into my living room with hats and replica shirts, cheering and singing support for our teams. There is always a lively atmosphere, particularly if we have 'away' supporters with us. One poor Newcastle United supporter got bombarded with cushions and empty beer cans after they scored against us. It might not be quite the same as the real thing but at least we get to watch the game with some of the excitement of actually being at the match. I know my grandad would have approved.

🍀 Of course, although there's nothing like going onto the Spion Kop and cursing with the rest, a trip round to the Moorgate Hotel, Kippax, to watch a live match - beamed from Australia by courtesy of 'Sky', in the presence of thirty other blokes, is some sort of alternative. Television doesn't have to be a solitary sport; it can be an activity. You can talk to the screen and play the devil with the ref, go for a pee in the interval and discuss the merits of the last try with the man who is peeing beside you and, if you've got time, get a couple in.

People go on about television killing conversation, but it's not killed in our pub.

🍀 In the end, television survives best as what you think happened rather than what actually did happen. For instance, if you asked me how Barbara Woodhouse trained dogs, I would say that she blew up their bottoms, whereas my wife informs me that what she actually did was to blow up their noses. I also believe that I saw Mrs Thatcher on television on the day that Port Stanley was liberated, standing in front of the television cameras and doing the 'V' sign, not palms outwards as Churchill did, but up in the way that said "Up yours". People say I couldn't possibly have done. In reply, I just say "Rejoice".

🍀 In the beginning, there were photographic plates. When Europeans reached far off places, some of the tribes smashed their cameras for, they believed that when a person has your likeness they have possession of your soul. Times change. Now, very few people hold this belief. No matter how remote, most communities in the world now have television. Photographs didn't take control of the soul. There is a distinct possibility, however, that television will.

Exmouth farmer, Charles Pidgeon, put TV in the milking shed to encourage his cows to produce more milk, 1961.